Building E-Commerce Solutions with WooCommerce

Second Edition

Transform your WordPress website into a fully-featured
e-commerce store with the power of WooCommerce

Robbert Ravensbergen

[PACKT] open source
PUBLISHING community experience distilled

BIRMINGHAM - MUMBAI

Building E-Commerce Solutions with WooCommerce
Second Edition

First published: November 2013

Second Edition: December 2015

Production reference: 1211215

Published by Packt Publishing Ltd.
Livery Place
35 Livery Street
Birmingham B3 2PB, UK.

ISBN 978-1-78588-156-5

www.packtpub.com

Credits

Author
Robbert Ravensbergen

Reviewers
Matthew Allan

Rémi Corson

Nicola Mustone

Commissioning Editor
Priya Singh

Acquisition Editor
Manish Nainani

Content Development Editor
Arun Nadar

Technical Editor
Bharat Patil

Copy Editor
Tasneem Fatehi

Project Coordinator
Neha Bhatnagar

Proofreader
Safis Editing

Indexer
Mariammal Chettiyar

Production Coordinator
Arvindkumar Gupta

Cover Work
Arvindkumar Gupta

About the Author

Robbert Ravensbergen is an experienced e-commerce and IT manager. He has been working in several international roles for various companies. He's also a passionate writer and blogger. WordPress, WooCommerce, and Magento are the topics that he writes about.

Robbert released several books about Magento and WooCommerce for Packt Publishing during the last couple of years. Besides this, he's an important writer in the Netherlands and well known for his understandable books for beginners about WordPress.

Readers can reach Robbert on his personal blog at `http://www.joomblocks.com`.

I would like to thank the employees of Packt Publishing for making this new book possible. It has been a pleasure working with you again. Besides that, I would especially like to thank the reviewers of this book, whose inputs were very valuable in creating a better product. Thank you!

About the Reviewers

Matthew Allan works with a growing team of developers at Prospress to bring top-notch plugins and extensions to the WordPress and WooCommerce platforms. Some of Prospress' most well-known extensions are WooCommerce Subscriptions and WooCommerce One Page Checkout—both available from woothemes.com.

Over the past 3 years, Matthew has been reviewing WooCommerce books and developing new software for entrepreneurs wanting to jump into the e-commerce world and start selling online. Matt's experience in developing and supporting premium extensions for WooCommerce has informed his technical review for this book.

Rémi Corson built his first website in high school, where, after a few months, he realized he was teaching web languages to his own teacher. Then, he decided to build his own content management system called PHPforge, which was used by more than 5,000 users at that time. He finally switched to WordPress a few years later.

Formerly in the top ten of CodeCanyon's best sellers, the largest code-related marketplace on the planet, Remi worked on Easy Digital Downloads' early versions with Pippin Williamson, and joined WooThemes as a Happiness Engineer in 2013 before the acquisition by Automattic in 2015.

Rémi is a public speaker and code expert. He works on WooCommerce core code on a daily basis and he built/refactored many official add-ons. He was also involved in the first WooConf organization in San-Francisco in 2014, the major WooCommerce-related event. Rémi writes weekly posts on his blog, mainly about WooCommerce, and provides a lot of free plugins and snippets.

He is also passionate about woodworking, surfing, and video making, and is a great guitar player.

Nicola Mustone is a web developer based in Italy, where he studied economy and programming. He developed his first website at the age of 15. Since then, he fell in love with programming and web developing, so he started studying it in depth, improving his skill set.

He started working as a freelancer at the age of 19. In 2011, he accepted his first job at a local web agency.

In 2012, Nicola moved from his birth city, Lucera, to Acireale in Sicily to work with Your Inspiration where he learned about WordPress in its entirety, from end user usage to themes and plugins development. Working at Your Inspiration, he specialized in WordPress development and customer support.

In October 2014, he started working for WooThemes, and in June 2015, Automattic acquired WooThemes. He is currently an automattician working in the WooCommerce support team as an Internal Support Ninja. Nicola also writes articles and tutorials regularly to help customers understand WooCommerce and WordPress better.

www.PacktPub.com

Support files, eBooks, discount offers, and more

For support files and downloads related to your book, please visit www.PacktPub.com.

Did you know that Packt offers eBook versions of every book published, with PDF and ePub files available? You can upgrade to the eBook version at www.PacktPub.com and as a print book customer, you are entitled to a discount on the eBook copy. Get in touch with us at service@packtpub.com for more details.

At www.PacktPub.com, you can also read a collection of free technical articles, sign up for a range of free newsletters and receive exclusive discounts and offers on Packt books and eBooks.

https://www2.packtpub.com/books/subscription/packtlib

Do you need instant solutions to your IT questions? PacktLib is Packt's online digital book library. Here, you can search, access, and read Packt's entire library of books.

Why subscribe?

- Fully searchable across every book published by Packt
- Copy and paste, print, and bookmark content
- On demand and accessible via a web browser

Free access for Packt account holders

If you have an account with Packt at www.PacktPub.com, you can use this to access PacktLib today and view 9 entirely free books. Simply use your login credentials for immediate access.

Table of Contents

Preface

Back in the early days of WordPress, the platform was mainly used to create and run blogs. Soon plugins became available to add functionality to the platform. A couple of e-commerce plugins became available as well. However, often they were incomplete or buggy.

In 2011, the WooCommerce plugin became available on the market, developed by the popular creators of Woothemes.com, where you can buy premium WordPress themes. WooCommerce was an instant hit and reached over ten thousand downloads in the first couple of weeks. A few years later, the plugin was downloaded almost 1.4 million times and it received a complete makeover during 2013 with the release of WooCommerce 2.0. Meanwhile, the solution has become mature and is even used for larger online stores.

The reason that the plugin became so popular is that it is so easy to use. Millions of people were already using WordPress for their blogs and websites and were looking for an easy way to be able to sell products and services directly on their own website. WooCommerce made this possible for all of us.

This book will explain you how to set up WooCommerce, create products, and use payment and shipping methods. You will work with themes and add plugins to expand the functionality of WooCommerce. It will teach you how to create and run your own online store in a very easy, straightforward manner.

It's time to get started!

What this book covers

Chapter 1, Setting Up WooCommerce, shows you how to set up a test environment and install WooCommerce. After that, you'll learn how to set up WooCommerce and work with taxes.

Chapter 2, Creating Your First Products, helps you create your very first products. You'll learn what the minimum steps are to get your products available and be able to start selling them.

Chapter 3, Using Downloadable Products and Variations, offers various other possibilities when creating products. In this chapter, you'll create downloadable products, learn how to work with attributes, and create variable products.

Chapter 4, Payments, Shipping, and Coupons, shows you how to set up payment and shipping methods for your store. You will also learn how to use discount coupon codes for marketing purposes.

Chapter 5, Working with WooCommerce Themes, shows you what you need to pay attention to and where to buy or download good themes. Having a solid WordPress theme available for your WooCommerce store is very important.

Chapter 6, Customizing a WooCommerce Theme, gives you a brief introduction to themes to get you started. Creating a WordPress and WooCommerce theme is worth a book by itself. You'll actually make code changes to your theme and find some practical examples.

Chapter 7, Running Your Online Store, starts with explaining how to bring a development store live. What do you do when the first orders flow in? How do you use WooCommerce to make sure that orders are handled correctly? We'll also show how to manually create an order and speak about reporting. Time to bring your store online and start selling!

Chapter 8, More Possibilities Using Plugins, explains which plugins to use and where to look for other possibilities. WooCommerce is a plugin for WordPress. On top of WooCommerce, you can install additional plugins to expand or change the functionality. But there are so many options, which plugins are a good choice?.

What you need for this book

In this book, we're assuming that you're familiar with using WordPress. You do not need development skills, but just a basic user-level knowledge of WordPress should be sufficient. Your WordPress website should be a self-hosted one. Using WordPress.com is not an option as it does not offer the possibility to install your own WordPress plugins.

If you're not yet familiar with WordPress, we highly recommend that you read one of the WordPress beginner's books or tutorials first. *WordPress 4.x Complete* from *Packt Publishing* is a good start (`https://www.packtpub.com/web-development/wordpress-40-complete`).

If you're already working with WordPress, we're also assuming that you know how to work with an FTP tool, like the free FileZilla.

Besides this, it's handy to have image manipulation software available, such as Photoshop, Photoshop Elements, Fireworks, or Gimp.

Finally, you'll need a code editor if you want to be able to change or create your own WooCommerce themes, a topic that we'll cover in *Chapter 6, Customizing a WooCommerce Theme*. Well-known editors are Notepad++ for Windows users and Coda or Sublime Text for Mac users. There are plenty of alternatives as well; just use the tools that you like.

Who this book is for

This book has been written for everyone who wants to learn how to expand an existing WordPress website with e-commerce functions using the WooCommerce plugin.

WooCommerce is an easy-to-use, but fully-functional, e-commerce plugin that will turn your website into a fully-featured online store. The book is suitable for marketers, e-commerce (project) managers, and web design agencies working with WordPress. First of all, this book is meant for everyone willing to run their own online store on a relatively small budget.

Although this book is not aimed at developers, some WooCommerce code examples are provided in this book.

Conventions

In this book, you will find a number of styles of text that distinguish between different kinds of information. Here are some examples of these styles, and an explanation of their meaning.

Code words in text, database table names, folder names, filenames, file extensions, pathnames, dummy URLs, user input, and Twitter handles are shown as follows: "Next, simply enter WooCommerce in the Search Plugins field and hit *Enter*."

A block of code is set as follows:

```
add_action( 'get_header', 'remove_storefront_sidebar' );
function remove_storefront_sidebar() {
  if ( is_product() ) {
    remove_action( 'storefront_sidebar', 'storefront_get_sidebar',
      10 );
  }
}
```

New terms and **important words** are shown in bold. Words that you see on the screen, in menus or dialog boxes for example, appear in the text like this: "Click on **Plugins** in the menu on the left-hand side, and click on **Add New**".

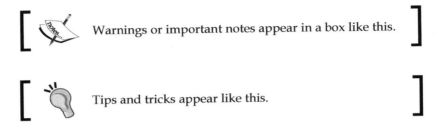

Warnings or important notes appear in a box like this.

Tips and tricks appear like this.

Reader feedback

Feedback from our readers is always welcome. Let us know what you think about this book—what you liked or may have disliked. Reader feedback is important for us to develop titles that you really get the most out of.

To send us general feedback, simply send an e-mail to feedback@packtpub.com, and mention the book title via the subject of your message.

If there is a topic that you have expertise in and you are interested in either writing or contributing to a book, see our author guide on www.packtpub.com/authors.

Customer support

Now that you are the proud owner of a Packt book, we have a number of things to help you to get the most from your purchase.

Errata

Although we have taken every care to ensure the accuracy of our content, mistakes do happen. If you find a mistake in one of our books—maybe a mistake in the text or the code—we would be grateful if you would report this to us. By doing so, you can save other readers from frustration and help us improve subsequent versions of this book. If you find any errata, please report them by visiting http://www.packtpub.com/submit-errata, selecting your book, clicking on the **errata submission form** link, and entering the details of your errata. Once your errata are verified, your submission will be accepted and the errata will be uploaded on our website, or added to any list of existing errata, under the Errata section of that title. Any existing errata can be viewed by selecting your title from http://www.packtpub.com/support.

Piracy

Piracy of copyright material on the Internet is an ongoing problem across all media. At Packt, we take the protection of our copyright and licenses very seriously. If you come across any illegal copies of our works, in any form, on the Internet, please provide us with the location address or website name immediately so that we can pursue a remedy.

Please contact us at copyright@packtpub.com with a link to the suspected pirated material.

We appreciate your help in protecting our authors, and our ability to bring you valuable content.

Questions

You can contact us at questions@packtpub.com if you are having a problem with any aspect of the book, and we will do our best to address it.

1
Setting Up WooCommerce

During the last couple of years, WordPress has outgrown any other Content Management Solution worldwide. Numerous websites are built using WordPress on a daily basis. WordPress is even popular among large companies. Currently about a quarter of all websites worldwide are powered by WordPress.

WooCommerce is a plugin for WordPress that turns your website into a complete online store. Practically in minutes, but that doesn't mean that the solution is very limited. This book will show you what you can do with it. WooCommerce is a versatile plugin that gives the possibility for everyone with a little WordPress knowledge to start their own online store.

Originally, WooCommerce was derived from the Jigoshop plugin. The WordPress theme developers of WooThemes quickly brought the solution to a higher level and soon it became the most popular plugin for e-commerce within WordPress. In 2015, Automattic (the company behind WordPress) acquired WooThemes and WooCommerce. So we could almost say that WooCommerce has become the default ecommerce solution for WordPress now. At time of print WooCommerce is even powering 30% of all online stores worldwide.

In case you are not familiar with WordPress at all, this book is not the first one you should read. No worries though, WordPress isn't that hard to learn and there are a lot of online possibilities resources to learn about WordPress solution very quickly. Or just turn to one of the many printed books on WordPress that are available.

The following are the topics covered in this chapter:

- Setting up your test environment
- Installing and activating WooCommerce
- Using all WooCommerce settings
- Setting up Tax
- Adding WooCommerce pages to your WordPress menu

Setting up your test environment

Before we start, remember that it's only possible to install your own plugins if you're working in your own WordPress installation. This means that users that are running a website on WordPress.com will not be able to follow along. It's simply impossible in that environment to install plugins yourself. WooCommerce has recently become a part of WordPress itself. I can imagine that because of this WooCommerce might become available for WordPress.com users in the future. But so far there are no signs yet of an integration of WooCommerce into WordPress.com.

When starting with WooCommerce there are two situations that might occur:

- You have a running WordPress website to which you'd like to add WooCommerce
- You want to start from scratch and create a new WordPress installation including WooCommerce

Either way, you'll need a test environment to be able to play with WooCommerce and follow along with this book. Although technically possible to add WooCommerce to an existing WordPress website immediately, I highly recommend using a test environment. Things can and will go wrong and you don't want to confront your current visitors with your experiments.

Setting up a WordPress test environment isn't as difficult as it might seem. There are tons of tutorials available, whether you're working on Windows or working with a Mac. When you want to add WooCommerce to your existing website, this is what you need to do to setup a test environment:

1. Create a backup copy of your complete WordPress environment using FTP. Alternatively use a plugin to store a copy into your Dropbox folder automatically: `http://wordpress.org/plugins/wordpress-backup-to-dropbox`. There are lots of solutions available, just pick your own favorite. UpDraftPlus is another option and delivers a complete backup solution as well: `http://wordpress.org/plugins/updraftplus/`.

2. Don't forget to backup your WordPress database as well. You may do this using a tool like phpMyAdmin and create an export from there. But also in this case, there are plugins that make life easier. The UpDraftPlus plugin mentioned above can perform this task as well. The steps 1 and 2 aren't necessary when you're starting a new WordPress installation from scratch.

3. Once your backups are complete, install XAMPP on a local (Windows) machine: `http://www.apachefriends.org`. Although XAMPP is available for Mac users, MAMP is a widely used alternative for this group: `http://www.mamp.info/en/index.html`. Restore your WordPress backup on your test server by copying all files to a subfolder and by restoring the database using phpMyAdmin.

4. Note that after restoring your database using phpMyAdmin, it's necessary to update the contents of the database as well. Unfortunately WordPress stores the full path URLs in lots of different database records. Without changes, those would still point to the location of your live website and not to your test environment. I mostly use a 'Search and replace' script to solve this issue. `https://interconnectit.com/products/search-and-replace-for-wordpress-databases/`. You can download the script, and store the contents of the zip file in a new subfolder of your test environment. Start it from there, like in the screenshot below. Next, replace the old URL with the new one from your test environment:

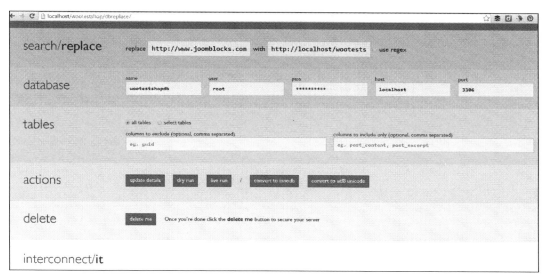

Alternatively, install a copy of your WordPress website as a temporary subdomain at your hosting provider. For instance, if my website is `http://www.example.com`, I could easily create a copy of my site in `http://test.example.com`. Possibilities may vary, depending on the hosting package you have with your hosting provider. Also in this scenario you need to adjust the content of the database, as mentioned in step four above.

If in your situation it isn't needed to add WooCommerce to an existing WordPress site, of course you may also start from scratch. Just install WordPress on a local test server or install it at your hosting provider.

To keep our instructions in this book as clear as possible we did just that, so that there's no visible interference with already existing content and a custom theme. We created a fresh installation of WordPress version 4.2. Below you see a screenshot of our setup, still completely empty using the Twenty Fifteen default theme:

More information about setting up a test environment and restoring your website on it can be found in the following articles:

- `http://wpsites.net/wordpress-tips/how-to-restore-your-wordpress-website-backup-on-your-local-server-using-wamp/`

- `https://codex.wordpress.org/Installing_WordPress_Locally_on_Your_Mac_With_MAMP`

- `http://code.tutsplus.com/tutorials/migrating-wordpress-across-hosts-servers-and-urls--wp-20104`

More tutorials will also be available on our website: `http://www.joomblocks.com`. Don't forget to sign up for the free Newsletter, that will bring you even more news and tutorials on WordPress, WooCommerce and other Open Source software solutions!

Once ready, we'll be able to take the next step and install the WooCommerce plugin. Let's take a look at our WordPress back-end. In our situation we can open this by browsing to `http://localhost/wootestshop/wp-admin`. Depending on the choices you made above for your test environment, your URL could be different.

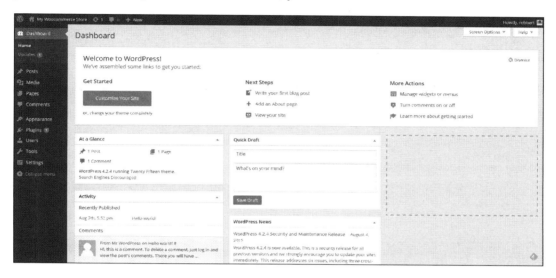

Well, this should all be familiar for you already. Again, your situation might look different, depending on your theme or the number of plugins that are already active for your website.

Installing WooCommerce

Installing a plugin is a fairly simple task:

1. Click on **Plugins** in the menu on the left and click on **Add New**.

2. Next, simply enter `WooCommerce` in the Search Plugins field and hit *Enter*.

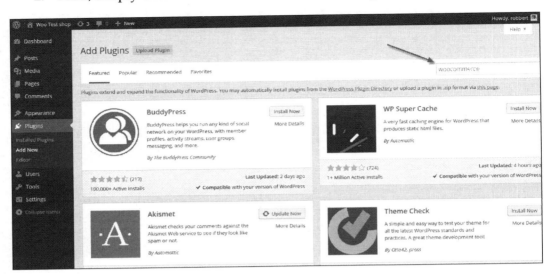

3. Verify if the correct plugin is shown on top and click **Install Now**. Over time results will vary, but the WooCommerce plugin itself should always appear on top:

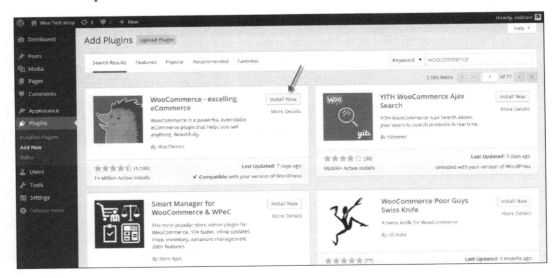

4. Click on **Activate Plugin**. Note that in the shown screenshot, we're installing version 2.4.8 of WooCommerce. New versions will follow rather quickly, so you might already see a higher version number:

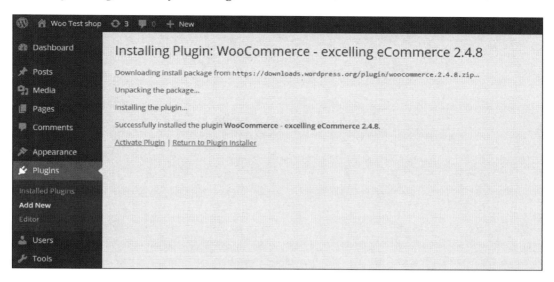

5. Next, WooCommerce starts a quick setup wizard, that gives the possibility to go through the most important settings. The wizard is optional. If you'd like to skip it just press **Not right now**, otherwise click the **Let's go button**. If you chose to skip the wizard, please read on at number 11 of this step-by-step guide.

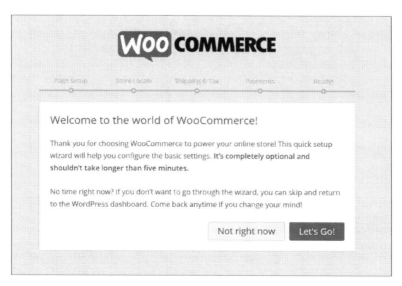

6. When using the wizard, first a couple of pages will be created by WooCommerce. These pages are necessary to correctly run your store, so just press **Continue**:

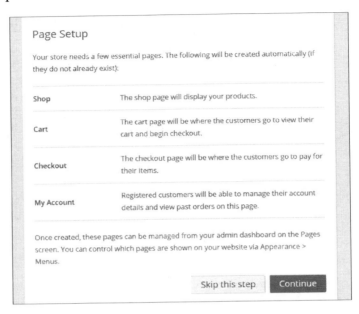

7. Next, choose your local settings, like the country you're based in and the currency you want to use. Also, set the units of measure, even if you think you won't need those for your products:

8. Set some basic shipping costs and determine how you want to work with taxes. Don't worry if you're still unsure here. You may **Skip this step** if you want to. Later on in this chapter these topics will be discussed in more detail:

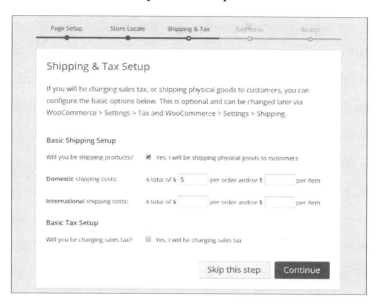

If you enable the checkbox **Yes, I will be charging sales tax**, additional options will become visible. WooCommerce will suggest some default tax settings, based on the country/region you selected at step 7:

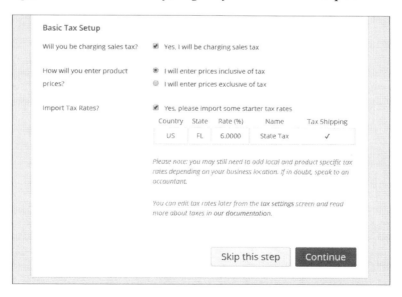

9. In the next screen, you can decide which of the default available payment methods you'd like to use. PayPal is widely used and adding your PayPal e-mail address is enough to start using it. Also in here, you may skip the step if you're unsure about it. Adding other payment possibilities than the ones shown here will be discussed later on:

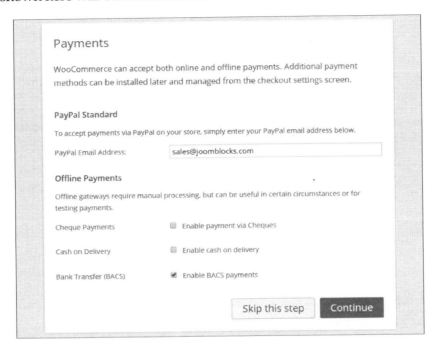

10. In the last step you're asked if you want to allow WooCommerce to gather diagnostic data of your store. If you do, you'll receive a discount coupon for extensions, which might be handy later on. Of course this step is optional. We recommend to click on the link **Return to the WordPress Dashboard** on the bottom. Although it is possible to immediately start adding products, we suggest to first pay more attention to the other WooCommerce settings:

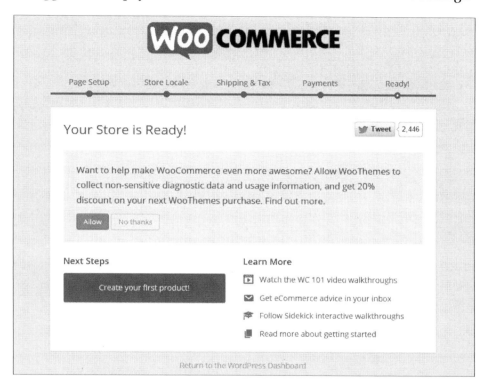

 In our example project, we're installing the English version of WooCommerce. But you might need a different language. By default, WooCommerce is already delivered in a number of languages. This means that the installation will automatically follow the language of your WordPress installation. If you need something else, just browse through the plugin directory on WordPress.org to find any additional translations.

11. Once we finished the wizard and returned to the WordPress Dashboard, two new menu items (**WooCommerce** and **Products**) have been added to the main menu on the left:

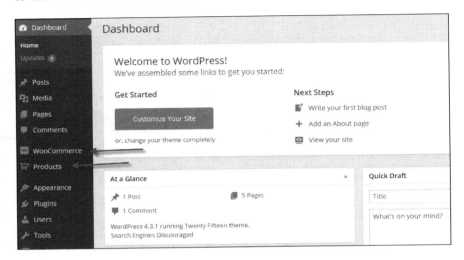

12. Meanwhile the plugin created the necessary pages that you can access by clicking on **Pages** in the menu on the left:

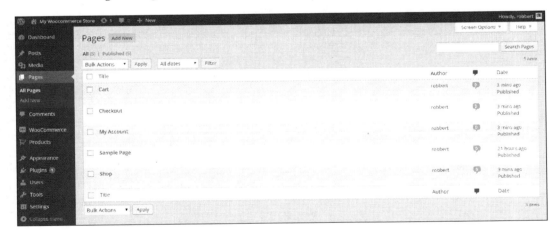

Note that if you open a page that was automatically created by WooCommerce, you'll only see a shortcode, that is used to call the needed functionality. Do not delete the shortcodes, or important WooCommerce pages like **Cart**, **Checkout**, and **Shop** will not work properly. However, it's still possible to add your own content before or after the shortcode on these pages.

Note that WooCommerce also added some widgets to your WordPress Dashboard, giving an overview of the latest product- and sales statistics. At this moment this is all still empty of course.

Setting up WooCommerce

WooCommerce is usable straight out of the box. However, in this section we'll cover almost every setup parameter that you may use to control your online store. Going through all settings might be quite overwhelming in the beginning, but it will help you in exploring the possibilities of WooCommerce.

The General Settings Tab

Click on **WooCommerce** in the left menu and then click **Settings**. A new page holding different tabs with settings appears. The first one visible is the tab named **General**:

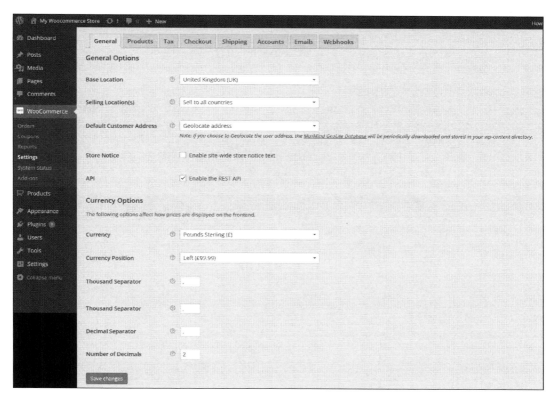

You will find certain fields described as follows:

- The **Base Location** holds the country of your store. The default setting may vary, depending on the country and language settings of your WordPress environment. Just change it if needed. Note that if you're in the United States, you'll also have to choose the correct state in this field. Note that the country field will be used as the default country for calculating taxes. It will also be used as the default country for customers checking out or creating an account.

- Next, determine to which countries you want to be able to sell at the field **Selling Location(s)**. Give it some thought, because enabling a country also means you must be able to ship to that country. If you set this field to **Specific Countries Only**, a new field appears in which you must select the countries that you want to allow selling to.

- At the field **Default Customer Address** you can decide how WooCommerce should set its defaults when a visitor wants to make a purchase. It can automatically set the country field based on the Geolocation of the customer, but of course this will only work if the customer is not working from behind an anonymous proxy. It's also possible to set the base address of the store as a default or no address at all. Why is this setting important? Because shipping costs and tax calculations might be based on the address of the customer. The better you're guessing the customer's location, the better shipping costs will be estimated immediately.

- If you immediately installed WooCommerce in a live website—which is not recommended— you have the possibility to show a warning message to your visitors. By checking the field **Store Notice**, the field **Store Notice Text** becomes available, giving you the opportunity to write your own text that will be shown on the top of your site:

- The next five settings are all used to set the way WooCommerce should handle your currency. WooCommerce is only able to work with one currency at a time. Set the desired **Currency** and choose where to show the Currency symbol.

- Finally, choose the **thousand separator**, the **decimal separator** and set the **number of decimals** you want to calculate with.

The Products Settings Tab

Moving to the next tab you'll find different settings related to the usage of products in WooCommerce. Note that this tab is divided into four different sub areas, starting with another **General** tab:

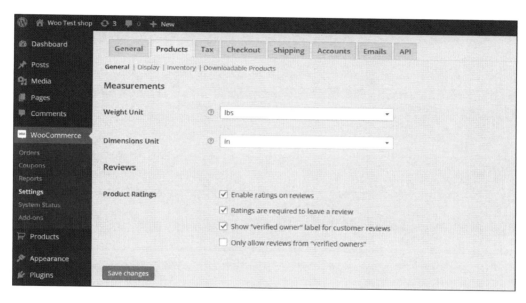

- First set the unit of measures for weight and dimensions.

- Next, check the settings for working with product reviews. You may choose to disable them, although generally that isn't recommended. Having customer reviews is important for almost all kinds of products and services. And even negative reviews are not always as bad as they seem to be.

- By default a user that wants to send in a review also has to give a rating to the product. If in your case that isn't needed, you might disable that setting.

- The last two settings here are used to show if a user posting a review actually bought the product in your store. You may also decide not to accept a review from someone that didn't buy the product in your store.

The next area, named **Display**, shows several settings for products and categories:

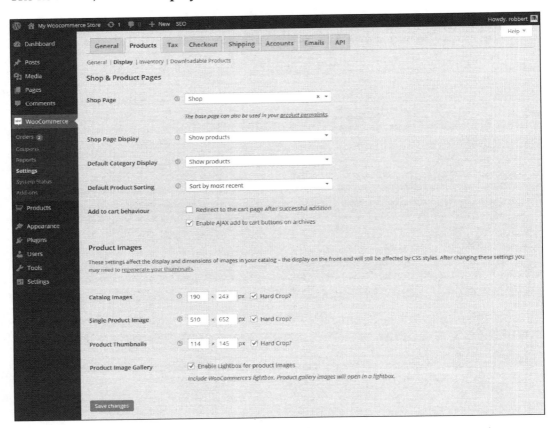

The setting for products and categories are as follows:

- The **Shop page** is already prefilled for you. Don't change it unless there's a real reason to. If you want to give this page a different name just go to the **Pages** menu and change it in there.

- Next, decide what will be shown on this shop page and on the product category pages. By default they will only show Products, but you can also choose to show (sub) categories or both. Of course a setting like this can be changed later on as well, so if you're unsure, just leave the defaults and come back later to try the different options.

- The field **Default Product Sorting** sets the way the products will be sorted in the front-end. Visitors have the possibility to change the sort order for their session.

- The **add to cart behavior** is important to understand, although also this one can be changed later on. The field **Redirect to the cart page after successful addition** is switched off by default. If you enable it, the user will be redirected to the cart page immediately when adding an item to the cart. This is especially useful for shops where in most cases the user will only buy a single product. If you leave the first setting disabled and enable the field **Enable AJAX add to cart buttons on archives** the page is not reloaded when an item is added to the cart. You may just try these settings to see what fits your store best.

- At **Product Images**, you define the size of your product images in the category overview, product detail page and thumbnail display. The uploaded pictures have to be at least as big as the highest value entered here. Take a little time to think about the right dimensions. Changing it later on is possible, but not that easy. The least you need to do is to decide if you'd like to keep the default square images, or maybe use photos in portrait mode. This highly depends on the products you are going to sell. Note: the theme you're using influences these sizes as well. You will read more on themes later on, but this might be a good moment to look at your theme documentation to find if it's mentioning anything about product image sizes.

- Keep the **product image gallery** enabled for a better, user friendly view of your images.

 If you change the image sizes after you created products or when using a new WordPress theme later on, the Regenerate Thumbnails WordPress plugin `https://wordpress. org/plugins/regenerate-thumbnails/` is very useful. It recalculates all images and image sizes at once.

- Press **Save Changes** at the bottom.

The next section shows various settings to manage the inventory of your products.

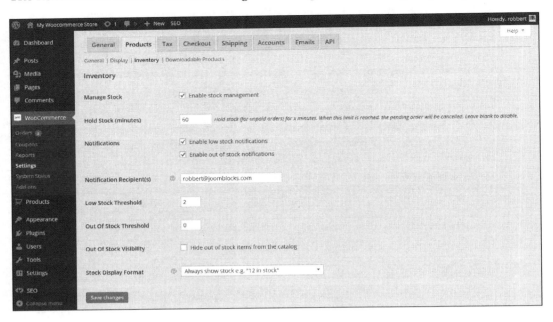

The inventory settings for the product page are as follows:

- First of all, set the **Manage Stock** field to **Enable stock management** if you want to work with inventory at all. If you're only going to sell services or downloadable products this might not be needed. If you're selling services as well as physical products then enable it here. It's possible to switch of inventory on product level later on.

- If you have limited stock available, you don't want it to be in a user's cart forever. On the other hand, once an item is in the cart you don't want to confront the user with a 'sorry sold out' message when they want to pay. The field **Hold Stock** gives you the possibility to influence the behaviour of WooCommerce in this area.

- When stock levels are important, you want to keep the **Notifications** field on enabled. Next, enter the email address these notifications need to be sent to.

- Next, set the **Low Stock Threshold** and **Out of Stock Threshold**, that will determine when the mentioned notifications will be sent. Unfortunately this is not a default. The settings chosen here will be the same for all of your products.

- Use the **Out of Stock Visibility** to decide whether or not to show products to visitors that are no longer available.

- Finally, set the field **Stock Display Format** to determine if stock levels are or aren't visible to your customers.

Remember to click the **Save changes** button at the bottom!

The last section holds some settings for downloadable products. If you're not planning to work with digital products you may skip this section:

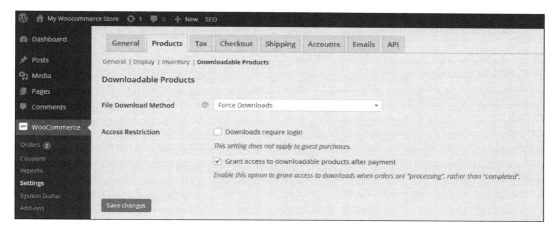

The options are as follows:

- Change the first setting **File Download Method** only if you have any issues with downloading the products by your customers.

- Next, decide if a login is required to be able to download an item using the **Access Restriction** field. Technically this isn't necessary, but you might have other reasons to force a customer to create an account on your website.

The Tax settings tab

Setting up taxes can be a difficult task. Of course there's no 'one size fits all' approach possible here. Tax laws and calculations differ from country to country and region to region. Besides that there's a large difference in handling taxes when selling goods to consumers or to other businesses. So in here we'll just stick to the basics, by explaining the functionality WooCommerce has available. It's up to you to find out how tax calculations should be done for your specific situation.

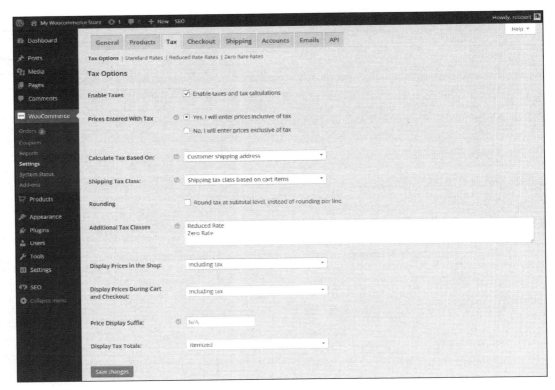

The settings for **Tax Options** page are as follows:

- First of all, decide if you want to **Enable Taxes**. It's not always necessary to display taxes in your store to your customers. If you decide to switch it off, you may ignore all other fields below.

- Next, assuming that you enabled the field above, decide if you want to enter your sales prices including or excluding tax in the **Prices Entered With Tax** field. Including tax is quite common in a consumer oriented store, but again, this differs per region.

- Depending on the tax rules in your country, you need to set the **Calculate Tax Based On** field. Sometimes taxes should be calculated based on the shipping address of the customer. In our example the base address of our store is used, which means that all customers will pay the same rate. By using the setting as shown, the applied tax rate will only depend on the product, not on the address of the customer.

- For the shipping costs, that will be discussed later on, you must also determine how the rate needs to be calculated. You set that using the field **Shipping Tax Class**. Although not always true, the default setting is often a good one, where the rate for shipping is the same as the one used for the item that is sold.

- WooCommerce works with a Standard tax rate by default. It's not possible to delete this one. You can add additional rates if you need them by adding a description of your choice to the **Additional Tax Classes** field. The **Reduced Rate** and **Zero Rate** have already been defined.

- The field **Price Display Suffix** may be used to display a short text just after the **Price** field. Use this to display for example *including VAT*.

- Once done, click on the link **Standard Rates** at the top of the screen to set your default tax rate. Click **Insert Row**. Just fill in the **Rate %** and set a **Tax Name** that makes sense for your customers. Note that it's possible to set rates per Country, State, or even based on Zip Code. Note that this will only work if you've chosen to base the tax calculations on the address of your customer! By default your Tax rate will also be used for the Shipping amount. Finally, using the field **Compound** it's possible to use multiple tax rates at once (tax on tax). Don't forget to hit the **Save changes** button:

Note that it's possible to import a CSV file with tax rates, which can be handy if you need to setup a lot of them. The **Import CSV** button brings you to the **Tools | Import** section of WordPress. Over there you'll also find the possibility to download an example file.

In a simplified way, assuming only one tax percentage applies, WooCommerce offers this method to calculate the tax amount:

Tax calculation for gross price (amount entered inclusive tax) is: *tax_amount = price - (price / ((tax_rate_% / 100) + 1))*.

Tax calculation for net price (amount entered exclusive tax) is: *tax_amount = price * (tax_rate_% / 100)*.

 When setting up taxes you might need to look up the two-digit country codes. Wikipedia has a good overview of all of them: `https://en.wikipedia.org/wiki/ISO_3166-1#Current_codes`. Wikipedia is also helpful when you need more information on tax rates per country: `https://en.wikipedia.org/wiki/List_of_countries_by_tax_rates`.

Setting up sales tax for the USA can be quite challenging sometimes. There's an easy solution for it, which is made available by WooTax: `https://wootax.com/`. Alternatively, have a look at the services offered by woosalestax.com (`http://www.woosalestax.com/`).

The Checkout Settings Tab

Moving on to the **Checkout** settings tab, we see again several sublevels. For this moment, we'll only discuss the **Checkout Options**. All other panels contain setup information about specific payment methods. More on choosing and configuring payment methods will be discussed in more detail in *Chapter 4, Payments, Shipping, and Coupons*:

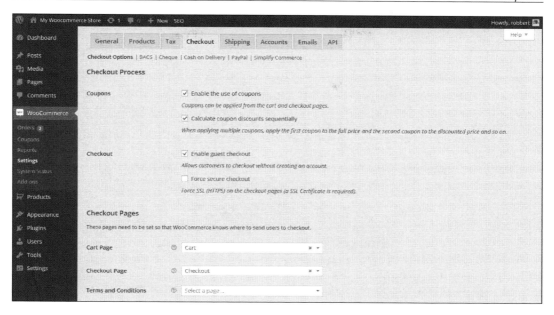

The **Checkout Options** are as follows:

- First, decide if you want **Enable the use of coupons** in your store. Using coupons gives a lot of marketing possibilities, but there's also a downside. Enabling this field will show a **enter your coupon** field on the front-end during checkout. Visitors will see the field and might start searching for a valid coupon on the web. In other words, only enable this setting if you're planning on using discount coupons.

- The next field is also enabled by default. Allowing a guest checkout has proven to be positive for conversions. Not everyone always wants to create an account for every store they buy something at. Having guest checkout enabled makes sure that these users can buy and pay without creating an account.

- The **Force secure checkout** field is used when working with SSL certificates. Enabling the field will mean that checkout is only possible when a SSL certificate is in place and a secure connection between the client (visitor) and the server (your website) could be made.

Not sure what a SSL certificate is and how to use that for your website? The principle cannot be explained in just a few sentences, but by using a SSL certificate on your website you'll be able to offer your visitors a safe connection during checkout. More and more customers pay attention to security measures like this. There are lots of companies that offer SSL certificates. Verizon (`http://www.verizonenterprise.com/products/security/identity/ssl/`) is a major player, but you may just as well ask your hosting provider for help. Especially if you need to be able to collect credit card information directly on your own website, using a SSL certificate is a must. In case you're using a payment service provider you do not really need one, but increasing trust is always a good thing. Besides that, the SSL certificate seems to become more important lately now that also Google considers it as one of the many ranking factors. So your website will rank better in Google if you have SSL enabled. More on payments will follow in *Chapter 4, Payments, Shipping, and Coupons*.

- At the **Checkout Page**, the first two fields have been pre filled again. You can keep them as they are. The third field, **Terms and Conditions**, is optional. If you want your customers to agree with your terms and conditions then do the following: save your changes here and head over to the **Pages** menu. Add a new page named **Terms and conditions** and fill it with your content. Save and publish that page. Next, come back here at the **Checkout** settings tab to select that page from the dropdown and save the settings again.

- The checkout endpoints were also automatically created. We recommend not to change these.

- Finally, the table with Payment gateways is shown and can be sorted here, but we'll discuss the usage of that one in *Chapter 4, Payments, Shipping, and Coupons*.

The shipping settings tab

Setting up **Shipping** works in a similar way as the **Checkout** setup. In here we'll show the **Shipping Options** and in *Chapter 4, Payments, Shipping, and Coupons* we'll get back with more detailed instructions:

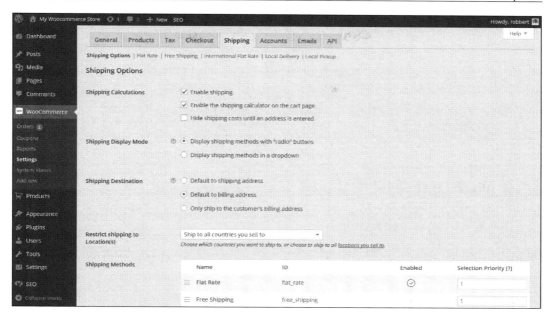

The **Shipping Options** settings are as follows:

- The first setting is enabled by default. It is needed if you want to be able to charge shipping costs to your customers. If you're only selling digital goods it isn't needed.

- Selecting the field **Enable the shipping calculator on the cart page** will result in the **Calculate Shipping** option appearing on the cart page. The customer will be able to calculate the shipping costs for a delivery to his location before continuing with the checkout process. The calculation is based on the country and zip code, which means that it's only useful if your shop offers shipping costs that differ per region. This is a handy function if you have configured your shipping options to apply different shipping costs based on the customer's region.

- The next option will do the opposite. If you enable it, the shipping costs will not be shown as long as the customer did not enter an address.

- The **Shipping Display Mode** just determines the way the shipping options are presented to the user: using radio buttons or using a dropdown field.

- The **Shipping Destination** controls which of the customer addresses is used by default.

- The field **Restrict shipping to Location(s)** gives the possibility to limit the number of countries you're shipping to. For instance if you want to sell digital products to all countries, but can only offer shipping of physical goods to a couple of them. By default, WooCommerce allows to ship to all countries that you enabled in the **General** settings tab.

- Next, you see the available **Shipping Methods**. It's possible to expand this list using additional plugins. More details on configuring your shipping methods will follow in *Chapter 4, Payments, Shipping, and Coupons.*

The Accounts Settings Tab

We're moving to the next tab, named **Accounts**. There are only a couple of settings here that you need to pay attention to:

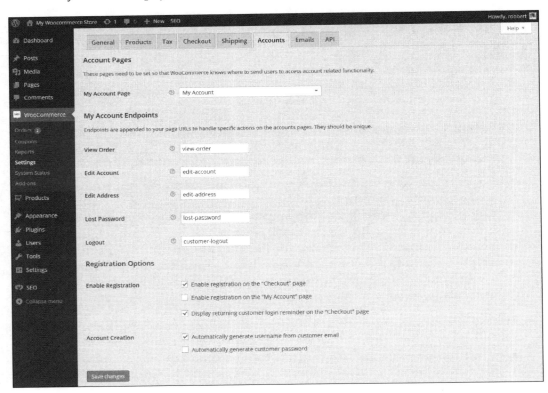

The setting for **Accounts** is as follows:

- The first part, **Account Pages** and **My Account Endpoints** may all be left at their default settings.

- The **Registration Options** deserve some more attention. First of all, you set where the customer can create a new account for the store. Make it easy and enable them both. Next, by default WooCommerce will show a reminder on the checkout page, so that existing customers remember to login.

- At **Account Creation**, WooCommerce can use the e-mail address as a username, or let the customer pick a username for themselves. The default option is generally the best one, because customers often forget the usernames they chose. Besides that the username must be unique, so in a large shop it could become a frustrating task for a user if the username of their choice has already been taken.

The Email Settings Tab

In this tab, you can configure the way WooCommerce handles e-mails it will send to your customer:

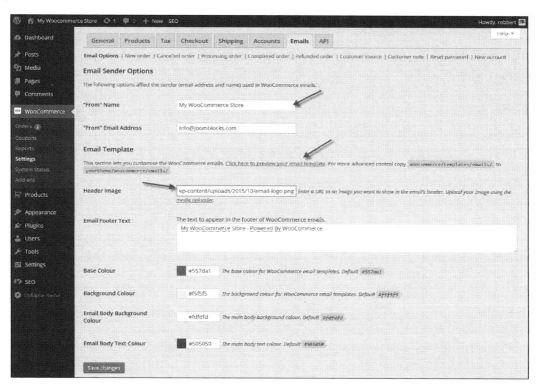

Also this tab contains several sub areas, starting with Email Options and followed by a couple of settings for every type of email WooCommerce can send:

- The **"From" Name** field is the name the receivers see in their email client. By default this is the name of your online store.

- The **"From" Email Address** field defaults to the administrator of the website, which defaults to the address created when installing WordPress. Of course this may be overwritten here.

- Next, if you want to you may add your logo as the **Header Image** for your emails. To be able to do that, do the following: Save any changes here and navigate to the **Media** menu. Upload your logo in the media manager. Open the image by clicking on it and copy the contents of the **URL** field. Go back to the WooCommerce settings and paste the URL in the **Header Image** field, like in the shown example.

- Feel free to change the default **Email Footer Text** field, which will be printed at the bottom of every e-mail.

- At the bottom of this settings tab, you have the possibility to change the default colors of the email messages, so that they fit to the colors of your website. Just click the color fields and use the color picker to change them. Or enter the hexadecimal color code directly into the field if you know the correct color codes of your website.

- After saving your changes, click the link in the middle of this tab to check the results. The shown e-mail message is empty, but it still gives you a good idea of how the messages will look like.

- If all seems correct, you can one by one check and change the settings of the various e-mails WooCommerce will send. The example below shows the settings of the **New Order** e-mail, which is the confirmation message that you will receive when your customer creates a new order:

Note: if you want to change more than available, you might need additional plugins or make code changes to the e-mail files yourself.

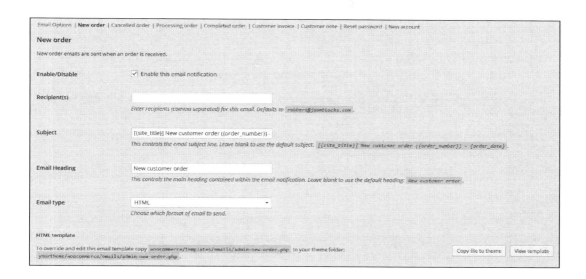

The API Settings Tab

The **Api Settings** tab is not discussed in this book. Api keys and Webhooks can be used to integrate third party tools with WooCommerce. Based on a trigger, another website or service can receive data from WooCommerce when certain events happen on your site, for instance when a new order is created. More information on Webhooks can be found here: `http://docs.woothemes.com/document/webhooks/`.

Preparing our test store

Now that we had a look at all settings of WooCommerce it's time to start adding products to our store. Before we do so, there are a couple of things that we need to do before moving on:

1. We need to add a link to our **Shop** in our menu. To do this, navigate to **Appearance | Menus** in the WordPress admin menu on the left. In your menu, add the **Shop** page to it. The simple example below shows a menu with only the home page and the **Shop** page assigned to it:

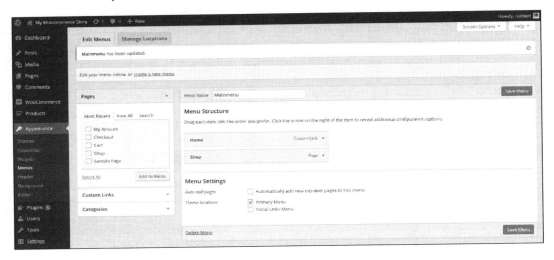

2. Since we are working on a clean installation of WordPress, it's wise to install a WooCommerce compatible WordPress theme. Don't worry yet if you have an existing website and don't know if your theme is compatible with WooCommerce—we'll cover that later on. Only do this if you started with a clean install and want to follow along. In our demo store we simply install the free theme named **StoreFront**, which is a standard and good starting point for new WooCommerce users. The theme has been developed by the developers of WooCommerce themselves. Navigate to **Appearance | Themes** and click **Add New**. Type Storefront in the search box and hit *Enter*. Click the **Install** button and activate the theme after installation.

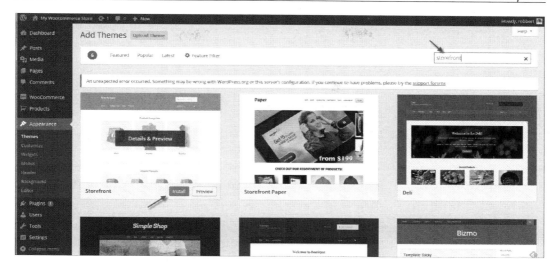

If you'd like to read more on installing WordPress themes you may use this link for a full tutorial: `http://www.joomblocks.com/installing-wordpress-themes`:

Summary

For this moment, we've covered the most important settings and we're ready to move to the next step. We've learned to setup a test environment and install WooCommerce, use the WooCommerce settings to setup our store in a way that fits our needs. Make the store available in our menu and install a WooCommerce compatible theme for our test environment.

In the next chapter, we will create our very first products.

2
Creating Your First Products

Now that WooCommerce is up and running and we had a look at its settings it's time to start creating a couple of products and build our online store. WooCommerce offers several possibilities to create your product catalog. In this chapter, we'll stick to the basics. You'll learn to:

- Setting up product categories
- Creating your first product
- Setting the categories, tags, and images for your product
- Learning about the other product types

Setting up product categories

When setting up your product catalog, it often makes sense to create **Categories** for your products, even if you have not so many products. Using a clear category structure makes it easier for your visitors to navigate and search your store. Further on you can use **Tags** and **Attributes** in your product catalog. **Categories** and **Tags** work in the same way you're used to from WordPress itself. **Attributes** are important for more complex product types. For instance, if I have a category for women's dresses, I could add **Attributes** for size and color. We'll discuss that in more depth in *Chapter 3, Using Downloadable Products and Variations*. Besides this, **Attributes** can also be used to add additional information to simple products.

For now, we'll just set up our category structure. Let's assume we are going to sell apparel in our store. We could start with three main categories in that case: Women, Men, and Children. If you're used to working with categories for (blog) posts in WordPress, you'll have no problem in creating them for your products. To create categories, perform the following steps:

1. Click in the left menu on **Products | Categories**. A form opens that lets you create a new category immediately.

2. Just fill in the **Name** of your category. If you want to you may change the **Slug** field that is used to create the link to your product category. If you do not enter a slug, it will automatically be created for you. In that case the category name is used, where spaces are replaced by hyphens.

3. Leave the **Parent** field to **None**. This is the first category we create, so automatically this field gives you no other choice.

4. You may use the description for your own purposes. There are themes that actively use the description of the category, but that isn't always the case. Note that WooCommerce does not accept the usage of shortcodes and/or HTML in the description field.

5. It's possible to add a thumbnail image to your category as well. Also in here, it depends on the WordPress theme whether or not this image is used on the product category page. If your theme doesn't show them, more experienced users can change the theme code to add them: http://docs.woothemes.com/document/woocommerce-display-category-image-on-category-archive/. Still in doubt? Don't worry, you can always come back later here and adjust the settings of your categories.

6. Hit the **Save** button to store the category.

Now that our first category has been created it's easy to add some more. Also we can create the next levels, by choosing one of the top categories for the **Parent** field. A simplified category structure could look like this:

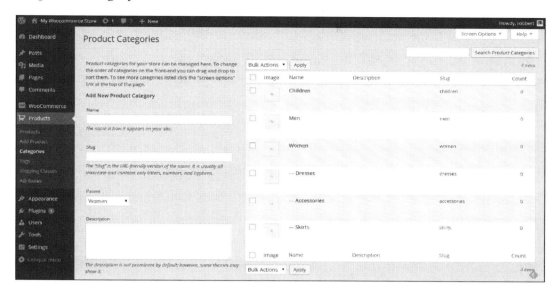

Creating your first product

Once we've created some categories, it's time to start entering our first product. Click **Products | Add Product** in the menu on the left. Looking at the categories we created, most of the products will require sizing and colors as well. That's something we'll discuss later on, so for now we are going to create a simple women's belt in the category **Accessories**.

In the example below you'll see that we already pre-filled a lot of information, just to give an idea of the fields you need to start with:

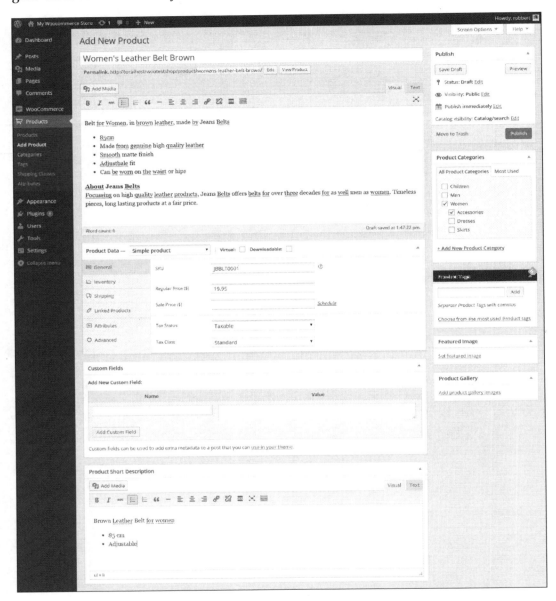

Let's have a closer look at all the available fields:

- Start with the product name on the top. Make sure to use important key words in this field. The permalink will automatically be created, just as with regular WordPress posts, but you may change it if you want to.

- In the editor underneath that, you may type the description of your product. Please note: this is the **long description**, which will be displayed at the bottom of your product page! The **Short Description** is more important, because that one will be displayed near your **Add to Cart** button. Strangely enough, this field can be found at the bottom of this page. You can move it to another spot on the page by dragging it, but you cannot move it above the long description. Also, in both description fields, make sure that important key words are mentioned to improve rankings in the search engines. It makes sense to fill both description fields at once and continue with all other product data after that.

- Below the description fields, there's an area containing a lot of fields that are important to understand. Using this area, you can control how your product will behave.

 If you want to do more on the optimization of your online store for the search engines, we highly recommend using the SEO plugin of Joost de Valk (Yoast). It's a general SEO plugin for WordPress, but it works fine with WooCommerce as well. You may find it here: http://wordpress.org/plugins/wordpress-seo/.

General data

The first tab in the area with product data is active by default and is named **General**. Just above that, you will notice that it's possible to select a **Product Type** and that there are two checkboxes available: **Virtual** and **Downloadable**. These are all items that will be discussed in *Chapter 3, Using Downloadable Products and Variations*. For this moment, we'll stick to the **Simple products**. These are suitable for anything that is a regular, physical product, without the need for the buyer to choose options or variables. For instance, a t-shirt available in different sizes is not a simple product, but a variable product. Let's take a closer look at the available fields for our simple product:

The parameters in the **General** tab are as follows:

- **SKU** stands for Stock Keeping Unit, also referred to as item- or article number. You may choose one yourself or just use the codes your supplier is using. Make sure to use a unique code. In most themes the **SKU** is also shown to the customer.

- The **Regular Price** is the sales price of your product, that your customers will see in the front end of your store. In case of a promotion you may use a **Sale Price**, for which it's also possible to enter a **Schedule**, so that the offer is only valid on certain dates.

- Depending on the settings you chose earlier in *Chapter 1, Setting Up WooCommerce*, for calculating taxes, you should choose whether or not the calculation of taxes is applicable for this product using the **Tax Status**. If a product is **Taxable**, also select the correct **Tax Class**. Using the **Tax Class** it's possible to work with different tax calculations, based on the type of product.

Inventory data

Moving to the next tab, we'll find a couple of settings that control the way we're handling stock levels for this product:

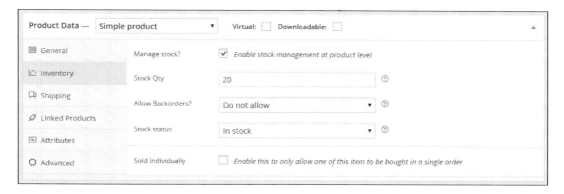

The parameters in the **Inventory** tab are as follows:

- First, decide if it's necessary to manage stock levels at all for this item. It's not always necessary to do so, if you've a small shop with only a couple of items. If you check the **Manage stock?** field, the **Stock Qty** field automatically becomes visible. In there enter the stock level you have available at the moment of creating your product.

- Decide if you want to be able to accept backorders from your customer if an item is no longer on stock. If you do, consider that customers might start asking you questions about the delivery date of the item they ordered.

- Next, make sure that the item's **Stock status** is set to **In stock**.

 Note: The product stock status can be used even if **enable stock management** is disabled in WooCommerce main products settings, which we discussed in *Chapter 1, Setting Up WooCommerce*.

- Finally, there's a parameter named **Sold Individually**. If you check it, your customers will only be able to add one of this item to their order.

Shipping data

Sometimes you need to be able to add additional information to your product, because shipping possibilities or rates might depend on the weight and size of your product.

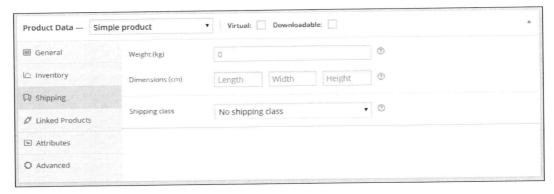

The parameters in the **Shipping** tab are as follows:

- Just enter the **Weight** and **Dimensions** if they are important for shipping, or if they are important for your customers to know. Note that premium carriers like for example UPS or FedEx require this information in most cases. The weight and dimensions are shown on the product page to your customer. Remember that the units of measure for the item's weight and dimensions can be set in the WooCommerce settings page.

- Select a **Shipping class** if the shipping rates are depending on the product that is being sold. More on shipping calculations will follow in *Chapter 4, Payments, Shipping, and Coupons*.

Linked products and attributes

Since this is our first product, we can skip the **Linked Products** and **Attributes** tabs for this moment. We'll use those later on.

We'll be using attributes a lot during the next chapter, when we'll be discussing more complex product types. The usage of attributes often even makes sense for simple products. Attributes offer a way to store structured product data in a way that it can be used for searching and filtering products. Instead of entering for instance the fabric as text, we could create an attribute for it. Using that method will give more possibilities to your customers to filter your product catalog. Besides that the attributes will be shown to the customer in the front end on the product page, in the **More information** tab.

Refer to *Chapter 3, Using Downloadable Products and Variations,* for more information on using attributes.

Advanced data

There are a few interesting fields in the **Advanced** tab:

- The **Purchase Note** will be included in any order for this product. It will also appear on the **Order Receipt** e-mail your customer will receive.

- Using the **Menu** order, you can influence the way your products are ordered. Note that this function depends on the settings you made during *Chapter 1, Setting Up WooCommerce,* If the **Default Product Sorting** field in your WooCommerce settings has been set to Default sorting, the **Menu order** field becomes active. You can enter any numeric value into this field, where the product with the lowest value will be displayed first on your shop page.

- Make sure that the **Enable reviews** field is checked. Having good, genuine reviews on your store is an important reason for potential customers to buy as well.

Setting the categories, tags, and images for your product

We're almost there now. Under the product data section there's a possibility to use custom fields that we also know from regular WordPress posts. We do not need that now. Always first try if you can solve your need using the standard available **Attributes** and **Tags**.

So far we've just used the main part of the product creation page. On the right there are the well known fields to publish the item. But before we do, we first need to take care of some other data, starting with the **Product Categories**. Just as with any regular WordPress post, just click the categories your product belongs to. Note that it's possible to select more than one category.

Next, set the **Product Tags** by entering them in the field and just press *Enter*. Don't use too many tags per product, stick to using a few. Having too many tags might lead to **duplicate content**, because the chance of having multiple pages with the same content increases in that case.

What is duplicate content? We speak of duplicate content if your website has the exact same content under two or more different URLs. You need to prevent that from happening, because search engines like Google won't know which page to show. The problem becomes bigger when people start linking to the different versions of the (same) content. Using too many tags for your posts increases the chance of having duplicate content. Joost de Valk from Yoast. com wrote some exceptional detailed information on this topic: `https://yoast.com/duplicate-content/`.

In the next screenshot you see an example of as well the selected categories as some tags that were entered for this product.

Below the **Product Tags,** there are two areas that allow you to add two of images to your product: the **Product Gallery** and the **Featured Image**. Before we start adding images, let's go back to the first chapter. Remember that we crossed a couple of settings that influence our image sizes? If you want to go back there now, first save your product as a draft and then go to **WooCommerce | Settings | Products | Display** using the menu. The image settings are on the bottom of that tab:

There are three image sizes that will be used by WooCommerce:

- **Catalog images** is the image that is used in your category and tag pages, when visitors are browsing through your product catalog
- **Single Product Image** is shown on the product page, showing a single item
- **Product Thumbnails** are only shown in your cart and checkout

It is important to use the same ratio for all three sizes. It's not mandatory to keep the width and height the same, the portrait format (where the value for width is smaller than the value for height) is often used as well, especially on fashion websites.

The check box at the field hard crop means that if you upload an image with a different ratio, they will automatically be cropped to the correct ratio as set here. This might mean losing a part of your image. Therefore it's always good to just prepare your images before uploading them to your website. Use the correct image ratio and use an image size that is at least as large at the dimensions of the **Single Product Image**.

Note: Not sure which values to use? Before you make final settings and start filling your product catalog with lots of items, it's important that you have set these values correctly. If you're buying a theme for a store, the documentation of the theme will often explain what to use. If you're creating a theme yourself, you're completely free in your choices of course. Sometimes it's necessary to regenerate all your product images, just because you changed the settings previously after you created your products. As also mentioned in *Chapter 1, Setting Up WooCommerce*, there's a plugin that can help you with this task: `http://wordpress.org/plugins/regenerate-thumbnails/`.

We're heading back to our product to start adding our images. The first and most important image is the **Featured Image**. Just add that by clicking on the link **Set Featured Image**. This will open your media library, just like you are used to from creating WordPress posts or pages.

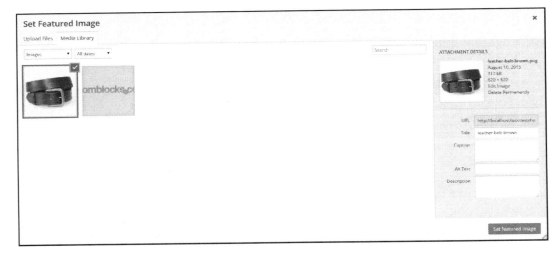

Click **Select files** and open a single image from your local machine. Don't forget to set a **Alt Text** and **Description**. Those are important for search engines! Then click the **Set featured image** button on the right. You'll return to the product maintenance page. If you have multiple photos available, don't hesitate to add those as well. Lack of good product photos is for sure a conversion killer. Click **Add product gallery images** and add the images you have available. Again, also for these images fill the **Alt Text** and **Description** fields. The result looks something like this:

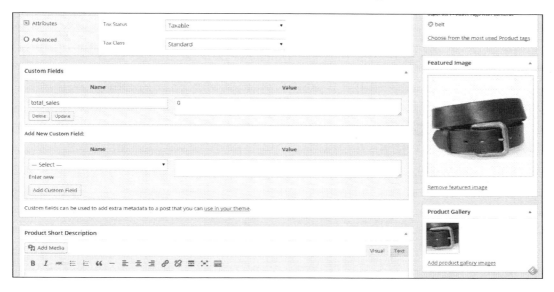

We finished the most important steps for our product and can publish it on the top right by clicking the button **Publish**. Of course we also want to have a look at the result in the front-end of our store. You may open the product page directly by clicking the button **View Product** on the top of the product screen.

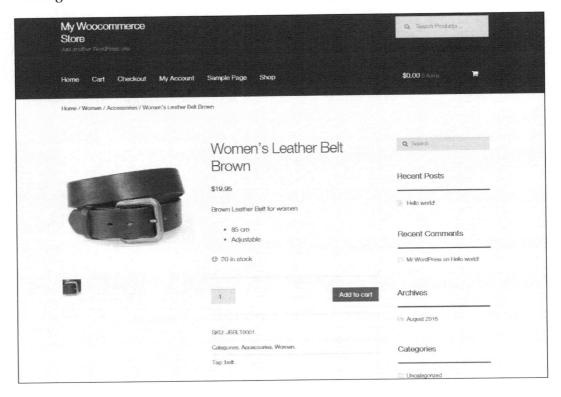

Since we are using the default Twenty Fifteen theme here, the layout of the page is okay but not more than that. Things could be better if we'd used an optimized WooCommerce theme. More on that topic will follow during *Chapter 5, Working with WooCommerce Themes*.

Product visibility options

When publishing our product there are some more options that we can use to influence the behavior of WooCommerce for this product. First navigate back to your product and edit it. On the top right we see several default WordPress fields, that we already know from regular posts like **Status**, **Visibility**, and **Published on**. The behavior of these fields is exactly the same as for a regular WordPress post and gives you the possibility to control if and when a product becomes visible.

Next, click on the **Edit** link near **Catalog visibility**, as shown in the following screenshot:

The default value, **Catalog/search** will have as result that:

- Your product is shown on the shop and category pages
- Your product will be shown in the search result if a visitor is searching for it

The other possibilities are:

- **Catalog**: In this case the product appears on the shop and category pages, but it will not be shown in search results.
- **Search**: In this case the product is not shown on shop and category pages. It can only be found by a visitor by searching for it.
- **Hidden**: A product with the value hidden will never be shown to your visitors and is only accessible if you know the exact URL. This can be handy if you would like to offer a product to for instance your e-mail subscribers, but do not want to make the product publicly available.

Just above the **Ok** button, there's a checkbox to make your product a **Featured Product**. **Featured Product** allows you to showcase specific products in different parts of your online store. You can for example show featured products in a slider on your homepage or in a widget. We'll show those possibilities later on in this book:

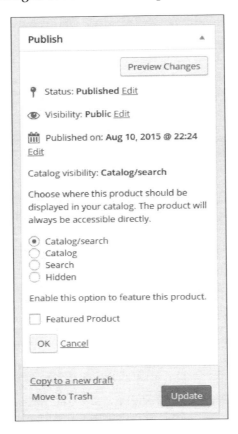

Remember to click the **Update** button if you make any changes to your product.

Summary

During this chapter, we have learned to create our very first products in WooCommerce. We have seen how to use the most important WooCommerce fields to determine the behavior of our product.

In the next chapter, we will be adding more complex products and learn how to use attributes to create them.

3
Using Downloadable Products and Variations

Our first product is available and we could easily continue using the same method to create multiple products in the same way. However, WooCommerce offers more possibilities than we just learned. In this chapter, we'll cover the following topics:

- Working with tags
- Virtual products
- Downloadable products
- Using attributes
- Setting up variable products
- Grouped products

Working with tags

We've mentioned the usage of product tags already in *Chapter 2, Creating Your First Products*. Using tags works exactly in the same way that you're used to when writing WordPress posts. So in here, we do not want to spend too much time in explaining the concept.

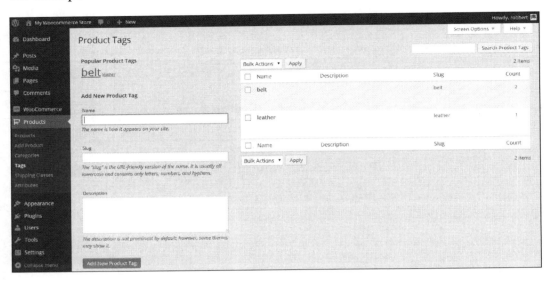

Just be aware that **Product Tags** and **Tags for Posts** are actually separated from each other. You may find the tags that you already used by navigating to **Products | Tags** in the menu on the left-hand side of your screen. Note that the tags that you entered during product creation appear here. Besides that, it's also possible to create a list of tags immediately in the **Edit Product** screen and use them later on. In general, when using a new tag, always ask yourself: *Will this be a tag that I'll use more often?*. If the answer is yes, go ahead and use it. If the answer is no, then it's better not to create that tag.

Virtual products

This product type is used for non-physical products. Use it to sell services, for instance. Virtual products will not be shipped, and as soon as you mark a simple product as virtual, the **Shipping** tab will disappear from the **Product Data** area. Besides that, if a customer only buys one or multiple virtual products in their order, the shipping address will be removed from the **Checkout** process:

Note: In the preceding screenshot, the **Virtual** field can only be set for a **Simple product**. If you need a variable product to be virtual, that's still possible but not using this field.

Downloadable products

If you have digital goods to offer to your customers, WooCommerce supports this using the **Downloadable** product type. Often, you'll also want to mark these items as **Virtual** since you won't physically ship anything. On the other hand, if your item will be as well downloaded as shipped, you should not check the **Virtual** field. An example could be a book that is physically shipped, but where the buyer also receives a downloadable copy.

Once the **Downloadable** field has been checked, new fields become available in the **General** tab. Click on **Add file**, followed by the **Choose file** button to upload, and attach a digital file to your product:

You may also set the **Download limit**, which determines how often a customer can come back to download the same item again.

Besides that, you can set the **Download expiry**. Fill in the number of days that the download stays available for your customer after purchase. By default, both fields are blank, which means that there are no restrictions and your customers can always come back to download the purchased items again.

 When using the **Download limit** or **Download expiry** fields, please note the following: if you ever need to change or replace an existing file, the download expiry and limit will be reset as it's technically a new file. Which means that the user can download the file again from their account or original e-mail.

Finally, the field **Download type** can contain the value **Standard Product**, **Application/Software**, or **Music**. If there's no fit for your product then leave it to **Standard Product**. This field controls the markup of your product page. To the end user, this field isn't visible, but it will tell the search engines what type of content the product contains. Unfortunately, the book type isn't supported in WooCommerce yet. More information can be found at http://schema.org/docs/schemas.html.

When your customer purchases a downloadable file, a link to download the item will be sent to the customer via an e-mail. But only if you enabled this e-mail in the WooCommerce settings. The link will also become available in the **My Account** section for that customer.

Whether or not a customer is forced to create an account in your store depends on the settings. Head over to **WooCommerce | Settings | Products** to check the settings for **Downloadable products**. See *Chapter 1, Setting Up WooCommerce*, for more information on these fields.

More information on using **Downloadable products** is available at the WooCommerce documentation website: https://docs.woothemes.com/document/digitaldownloadable-product-handling/.

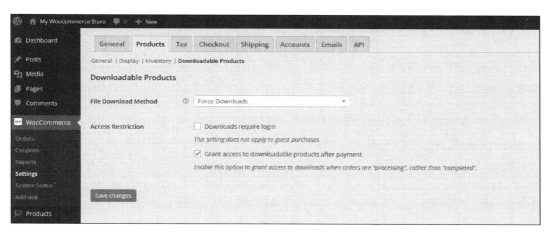

Using attributes

At first glance, attributes look like tags when we're accessing the function using the menu, **Products | Attributes**:

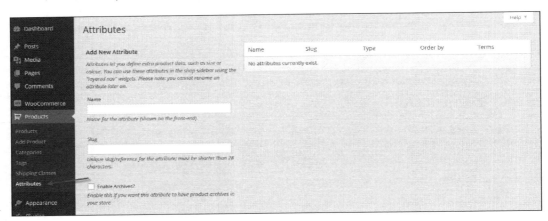

However, there is an important difference between **Attributes** and **Categories**. **Attributes** deliver a powerful mechanism to create different kinds of products. Besides that, working with **Attributes** is often smarter than working with **Categories** alone. **Categories** are used to organize entire products, whereas **Attributes** are a way of organizing product properties. Let's start with an example to clarify this.

Our simple product that we created earlier (the Brown Women's Belt) could easily be put in a category structure like: **Women | Accessories | Belts**. But that would give us all available belts in your store, right? And not just the brown ones. Ok, so we'll add another category for that! But no, although it is possible, it's not the best way to do it. Using **Attributes** in such a situation for the color is much more powerful. It will give your visitors the possibility to immediately filter all brown products once they're in the **Accessories** category so they can mix and match. Using categories for describing the color of your product is really a no-go. In other words, a category is a group in which a set of products can be bundled together. An attribute is a specific characteristic of a product. Other products may share that characteristic (for example, multiple products can be a `medium` size or have a `brown` color).

Since the usage of colors in our fashion store example is something that we'll need for sure, we are going to create that **Attribute**.

Creating an **Attribute** is very simple. Just enter the **Name** of the attribute (Color, in our example). You may leave the **Slug** field empty, it will automatically be filled based on the name of your attribute. Next, make sure that the **Type** field is set to **Select**. If you would set it to **Text**, it will give you the possibility to add values for every single product manually. Using **Select** will make sure that you enter and standardize the values beforehand. In most cases, using **Select** is the better choice.

The **Enable Archives** checkbox may stay switched off. This field allows you to create separate pages based on your attributes. So for instance, a page holding all the products in your store that are black. This can be handy, but also requires some additional coding to reach the desired result.

Leave **Default sort order** to **Custom ordering** so that later on, we'll be able to sort our **Attribute** values in the way we want to.

Click on the **Add Attribute** button:

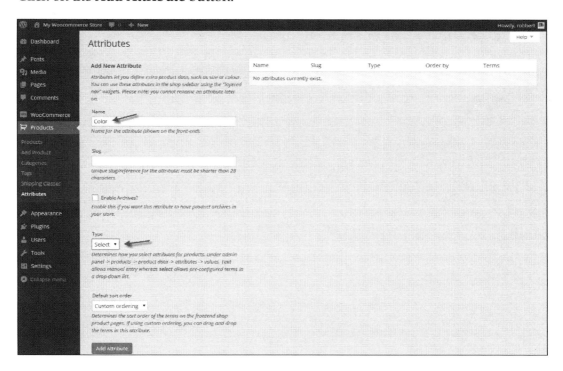

Now that our **Attribute** has been created, it appears in the table on the right-hand side of the screen:

Click on the button on the right to **Configure terms**.

Next, add all the colors that you will possibly need in your store. Don't worry though, it's always possible to come back later and add more. For every color, just enter the name and click on **Add New Color**. You'll soon have a long list of colors available. Remember that these colors will be used later on, when we're creating new products.

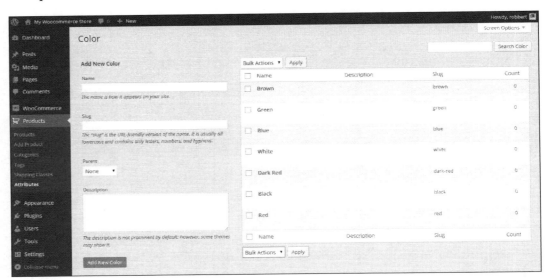

Once done, go back to the **Attributes** form again by clicking in the menu on the left. Now repeat the preceding steps and create a new **Attribute** named `Size` or `Shoe Size`. When working with sizes, there are a lot of different possibilities, so you might want to distinguish the sizes depending on the products that you are going to use them for. We create `Shoe size` to support our next example. Our result looks like this:

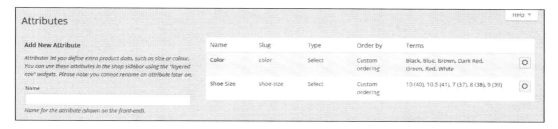

Now that we created some attributes, we'll be able to create a **Variable Product**.

The attributes we created here will be available for all products. That's a good thing for attributes that will be used often. However, on the product level, we'll see later on that it is also possible to add attributes which are used for that product only and not shared with others.

Setting up variable and grouped products

We've just created our first attributes that we'll use to add some shoes to our women's fashion store. Of course, we do not want to display all the sizes as individual products. We want to show our visitors one product and let them choose the right color and size. This is done using a variable product. To create a variable product, perform the following steps:

1. Start by creating a new product. Add a long and short description, select the correct category or create one, and assign a couple of tags. Set a featured image that will appear in your product category page.

2. Next, in the **Product Data** area, select **Variable product** as the product type:

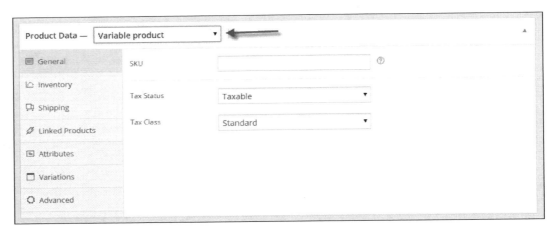

3. Note that some fields have disappeared; it's no longer possible to add the product price here. The **SKU** field is still available, but normally, you would leave it empty and set individual SKUs at a lower level. We'll see that in a minute. On the **Inventory** tab, **Enable the Manage Stock?** field, but do not set the **Stock Qty** field. Later on, we'll add the stock levels for individual products. Skip the other tabs for now and head over to the **Attributes** tab:

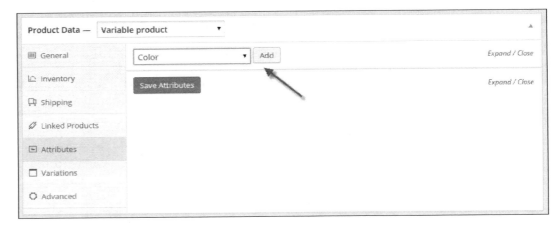

4. Click on the drop down that says **Custom product attribute**, select **Color**, and click on the **Add** button.

5. Next, check the fields, **Visible on the product page** and **Use for variations**. This will make sure that our visitors will be able to see this attribute, and we'll be able to create multiple instances (variations) of our product using different colors.

Note: if you would just select **Visible on the product page**, the attribute would become visible to the customer as a property of this item. But as information only, you would not be able to use that attribute when creating variations of your product.

6. On the right, click into the **Value(s)** field and select the colors that you want to use for this product. To keep things a little bit simple for our example, we just select `Blue` and `Grey`:

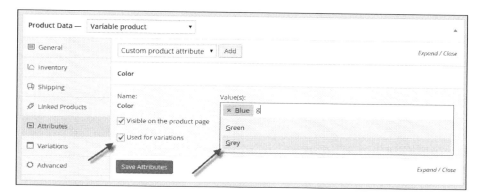

7. We repeat the same steps for our `Shoe Size` attribute, but now we push the **Select All** button to immediately select all the available shoe sizes. The final result will look as follows:

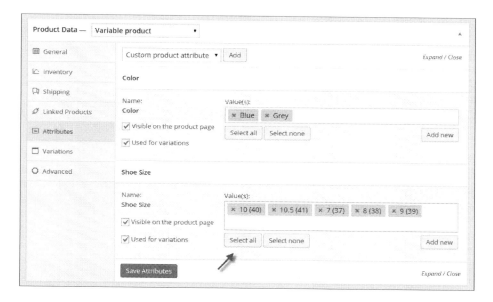

8. Click on the **Save Attributes** button on the bottom left of the **Attributes** tab. Or alternatively, save the draft of your product in the top-right corner of the product screen. Next, head over to the **Variations** tab. If you forget to save your attributes before moving on to the **Variations** tab, the following error message will appear:

9. Return to the **Variations** tab and note that now some fields have become visible. Click on the drop down and select **Create variations from all attributes** to assign all the possible combinations of colors and sizes at once. It's also possible to add them one by one in case you do not have all the possible combinations of the attribute values available. Click on **Go**:

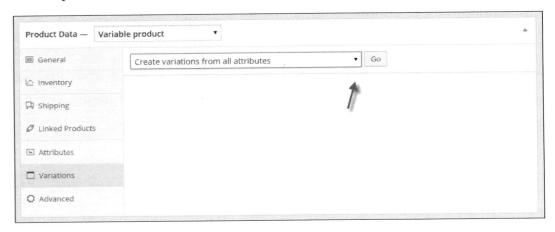

10. WooCommerce will give you a warning message because this may create a large number of combinations (two colors having five different sizes makes a total of 10 variations). Click on **Ok**. Another message appears mentioning the number of created variations. Click on **Ok** again.

There's a limit of 50 variations per run. Please note that you should not create too many variations. If you would have more than 100, the chances are high that you'll be creating a complex product for your customers. For more complex products, there are additional plugins available to support that. Refer to *Chapter 8, More Possibilities Using Plugins*, for more information.

11. A large area with all the variations will now be displayed. Click on one of the rows to expand all the underlying fields of that variation. Note that it's now possible to set a number of fields for every variation individually. The price may differ, the available **Stock Qty** may differ, and you can set an individual SKU for every variation. It's also possible to assign a different image per variation. Start filling in your variations individually. If a field is set to the value **Same as parent**, then the variation holds the same value as the parent item.

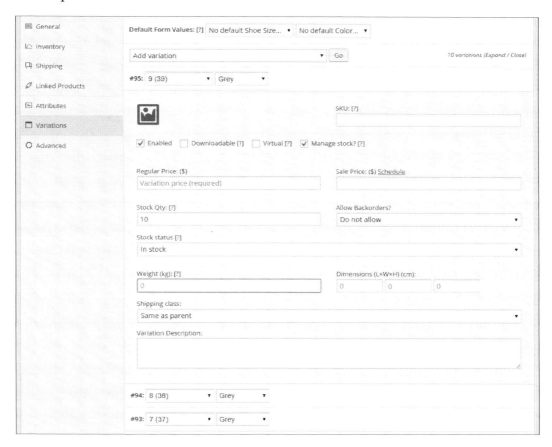

12. You may also use the handy **Bulk Edit** function on top to change fields for all the variations. That function is a bit hidden in the current WooCommerce version, but you may find it by clicking the drop down at the top that currently still says **Create variations from all attributes**. For example, when creating our demo shoe product, generally all the sizes will have the same sales price. We could enter them one by one for every variation, but it's much faster to do them all at once using the function, **Set regular prices**:

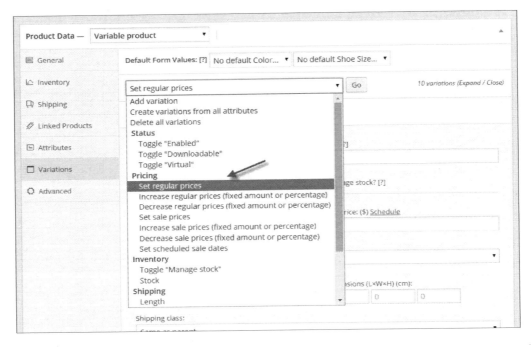

13. We normally work this way to set everything, we need, but your situation may differ depending on your products of course:

    ○ Set the field **Regular Price** for all the products at once using the **Bulk Edit** function.

    ○ Click on the little image area to set a separate product image per variation. In our demo product, we need this to be able to show a different image depending on the color that the user chooses. So, if the user selects the shoes in blue, we want that automatically the product image changes to the blue variation. You reach this by assigning an image to every single variation.

    ○ Set the **SKU**, **Image**, and **Stock Qty** individually for every variation, assuming that the stock quantities are not all the same.

- The following image below shows the **Bulk edit** option to change the regular sales price for all the variations at once:

14. The result should look something like this:

15. The last step that we have to take now is to publish the product in the top-right corner of the screen.

Note: if you made a mistake creating your variations, you can individually delete them by using the **Remove** button or use the **Bulk Edit** function again to delete them all at once. It isn't possible to set the image for all the variations at once, but be aware that, in fact, you only have to set this image for the variations where the image differs from the one that you set earlier as **Featured Image** on the main product level! If you do not set an image for your variation, WooCommerce will simply show the featured image of the main product.

16. Now that we published our product, of course, we want to see the end result in the frontend:

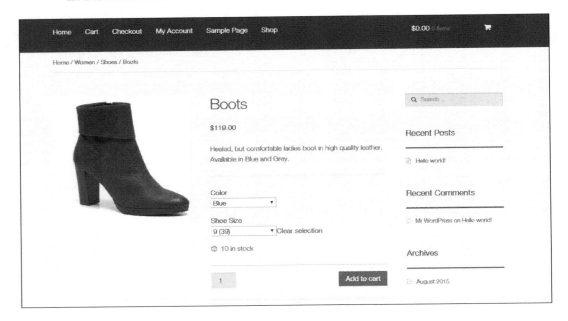

Note that the image that is shown automatically updates if the visitor selects a different color. If that doesn't happen, in your situation it's a problem of the WordPress theme and not an issue in WooCommerce. Are you thinking about changing the way this product page looks like? In *Chapter 5, Working with WooCommerce Themes*, we'll learn how to adjust the look and feel of our store.

You probably noticed that the **Add to cart** button does not become available if no variation has been chosen yet. To overcome this problem, you can set a default form value for your product in the backend so that it will be displayed immediately:

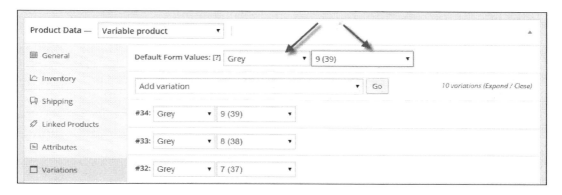

When working with a product with lots of variations, there's something important that you need to know about the product page your visitors see. Because of performance reasons, WooCommerce does not load the availability of all the variations if you have over 20 variations in a single product. In such a case, the attributes of the variation will be loaded using Ajax once a variation is selected by the user. This might mean that the user sees a certain color or size, but that it actually isn't available anymore. WooCommerce will show a message to the user in that case. Below 20 variations this issue doesn't exist.

Also in the WordPress administration, this limitation of 20 variations becomes visible. Pagination has been added on the top and bottom of the list with variations. This has been done to make sure that the number of items that must be loaded at once is manageable. Loading lots of variations was a former issue within WooCommerce, where products became very slow in the WordPress backend. This has been solved as of WooCommerce version 2.4.

Other product types

If you paid some attention to the screenshots earlier in this chapter, you would have noticed that there are even more product types available in WooCommerce. Besides Simple and Variable products, we can create the following:

- **Grouped products**: Think about a package, like for instance, a complete set that contains a computer, monitor, and mouse. Or a fashion set that includes a dress and matching shoes.

- **External/Affiliate products**: This is a special kind of product, which is actually sold on another website.

Grouped products

To create a grouped product, just simply select the type at the top of the **Product Data** area:

Fields that are no longer necessary will be removed. For instance, note that for a **Simple product**, there are various settings to control the stock levels. For a **Grouped product**, this isn't the case. You can only set the group to in stock or out of stock.

Unfortunately, it's not possible to set a sales price for the group. In your product catalog, WooCommerce will display *From $xx*, where *xx* is the price for the individual item with the lowest sales price. The final price that your customers pay will be calculated automatically, by adding the total sales prices of the individual products that your customer selects. In fact, the grouped item will display the individual items of the group together. Your customer is still in control of the items that will be put in the basket. Finish your product and create individual (simple) products that will belong to this group.

When creating the individual products for your group, please note the following:

- Do you want to sell this **Simple product** individually as well or only as a part of the **Grouped product**? Depending on your needs, set the appropriate value in the **Catalog Visibility** field in the top-right corner. In this example, I've set the visibility to **Hidden** so that this product can only be sold as part of the group.

- To link your individual product to the group, click on the **Linked Products** tab and select the correct grouped product by typing a part of its name:

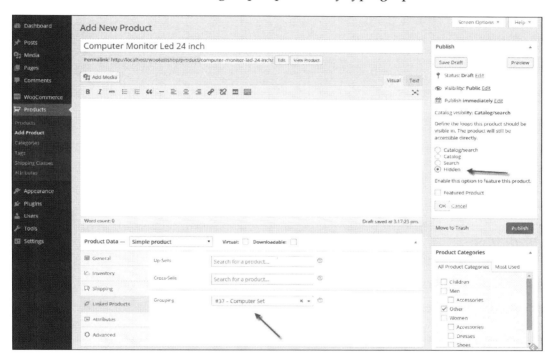

The end result of the grouped product in the frontend could look as follows:

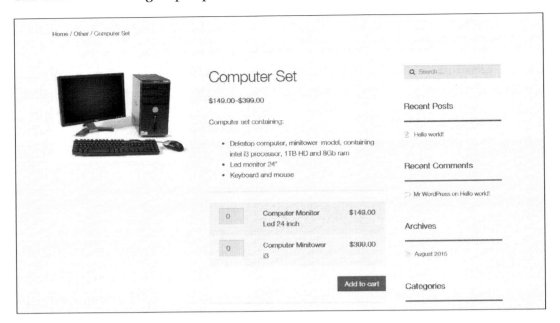

Note that the user has to enter the number of items he wants for every simple product. Often, that doesn't make sense. If you need more functionality for your grouped products, then you'll have to add additional plugins to WooCommerce.

External/Affiliate products

This last product type that WooCommerce offers is a special one. As you probably know, affiliate marketers promote products of other websites. Using this product type, you can create products that are actually sold elsewhere. As a site owner, you'll often earn a percentage of the sale. This product type is popular among bloggers since it gives them the possibility to monetize their blog without having to create a full featured online store and keep stock levels themselves.

When creating such a product, the **Product URL** is the most important field. It redirects the visitor to the store that the product is actually sold in, including a unique code. Using this code, the seller will know that this buyer came from your website and you will receive your affiliate fee if that customer closes the sale.

If you use your products in this way, the buyer will no longer be able to add an item to the cart. They will simply be redirected to the original store.

Note: if you want to use WooCommerce for affiliate marketing purposes, there are lots of possibilities to integrate with large Affiliate networks. Every country has its own affiliate partners available. Larger retailers have their own affiliate programs available, like Amazon.com for instance.

Importing product data

When you need to create a lot of products, it's good to take a closer look at the possibilities to import products automatically to your WooCommerce store.

The plugin WP All Import will, for example, deliver the possibility to import product data from XML and CSV sources (`http://wordpress.org/plugins/woocommerce-xml-csv-product-import/`).

WooThemes is also offering a plugin to import products using a CSV file named **Product CSV Import Suite** (`http://www.woothemes.com/products/product-csv-import-suite/`).

Both plugins have a similar price range. They aren't cheap, but they can save a lot of time if you need to create hundreds of products. Based on your needs, WP All Import might be a bit cheaper. WP All Import proves to be more flexible, especially if you're also working with the plugin Advanced Custom Fields. Or if you would like to use the plugin for other import tasks as well. It is a more generic import solution, where the Product CSV Import Suite is just used for importing products. A pro of the Product CSV Import Suite plugin is that it's also able to export data. Both solutions can do the job, so just check which one best fits your needs.

Summary

In this chapter, we've learned to create more complex products in WooCommerce. We need this to be able to create products with for example colors and sizes, but also if we're selling services or digital items. WooCommerce offers various possibilities using downloadable, virtual, variable, and grouped products. It's even possible to combine these techniques and create a variable, downloadable product.

If you need to create lots of products, there are various plugins available to help you getting the job done.

Now that we've covered everything about using products, it's time to take a closer look at shipping and payment methods in the next chapter.

4
Payments, Shipping, and Coupons

You now have enough knowledge of the product possibilities WooCommerce has to offer. You may continue to add multiple categories and products to fill your product catalog. Next, we'll need to take a closer look at the shopping process your customers will be offered. In this chapter we'll have a closer look at:

- Setting up Payment methods
- Using PayPal
- Using Stripe for credit card acceptance
- Setting the Shipping methods and prices
- Using discount coupons

Payment methods

Earlier in this book, during *Chapter 1, Setting Up WooCommerce*, we skipped the areas about handling the payment and shipping methods. These are both important subjects for your online store that deserve additional attention. Let's start with the payment methods that you'll offer to your customers.

Payment methods around the world

Which payment methods should you offer in your store? First of all, there's no best answer to this question. Looking at the payment solutions that are available worldwide, you might be surprised. There are literally hundreds of possibilities.

When speaking of payment methods, we distinguish between the following types:

- **Online or onsite methods**: the transaction is done online immediately at moment of creating the order by your customer. Payment by credit card or PayPal are examples of online payment methods.
- **Offline or offsite methods**: these payment methods do not authorize or capture the order amount online. In this scenario the user will pay in a different way, for example by doing a manual bank transfer or by paying at moment of delivery of the ordered items.

The methods that you need to offer to your customers will differ from country to country. Especially if you're selling locally (within a specific country), you need to prepare your store for that market. If you're not sure which payment methods you should offer, just look at the methods other online stores in your market are offering. Here are some, possibilities, but be aware that the list below only cover the most important, widely used payment possibilities:

- Credit Card
- Debit Card
- Bank transfer
- Cash on delivery
- Pay after delivery
- Cheques
- Online wallets

This list explains something about the payment methods, but not about the **Payment Provider** yet. A payment provider allows the online store to accept payments in different forms and will authorize the transactions. Often they also provide an online tool to manage your funds. Just to mention some of the major players:

- PayPal
- Amazon
- Google (Google Checkout, Google Wallet)
- Alipay (China)
- Credit card companies Mastercard, Visa, American Express, or Discover
- Stripe
- And many others.

It's important to understand the difference between a Payment Provider and a Payment Gateway. The Payment Provider is the company used to offer one or multiple **Payment methods**, which are in WooCommerce referred to as **Payment Gateways**. For example, PayPal is a Payment Provider, offering Payment Gateways like PayPal Pro, PayPal Express Checkout and PayPal Digital Goods. Often, a Payment Provider offers multiple Payment methods.

For your store it's likely that you need to offer a combination of payment possibilities. Let's first have a look at what WooCommerce has to offer by default. Navigate to **WooCommerce | Settings | Checkout**.

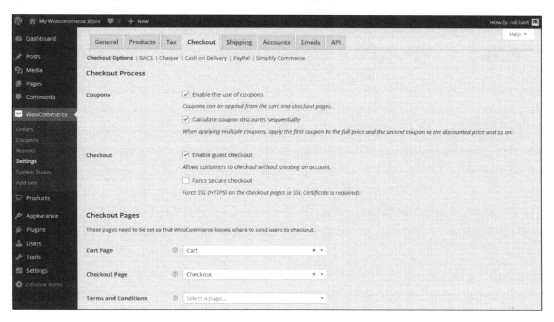

The **Checkout Options** were already discussed in *Chapter 1, Setting Up WooCommerce*. Note that next to the screen with options, we can see the following payment methods:

- **BACS** (Direct Bank Transfer)
- **Cheque**
- **Cash on Delivery**
- **PayPal**
- **Simplify Commerce**

In fact, the methods mentioned above are offline payment methods, except for PayPal and Simplify Commerce. PayPal is widely accepted. Simplify Commerce is at moment of writing only available for the USA and Ireland.

An offline payment method means that your customer can use that method if you offer it, but the actual payment is not carried out immediately. You'll have to manually check later on if you received the money from your customer. The offline method requires that your customer makes sure the payment is done. Online payment methods immediately do the payment transaction online, at the moment of sale. In most cases the payment is verified automatically and the order status in WooCommerce will be updated accordingly.

What you need to know about credit cards

When you want to accept credit cards in your store, you'll soon hear something about PCI compliancy. The issue is: if you let your customers enter their credit card details directly on your website, you must be PCI compliant. The downside is that getting your website PCI compliant is difficult to reach.

If you'd like to know more about this subject, the following website may be useful: `http://www.pcicomplianceguide.org/`.

So, how are we going to solve this? We still need to be able to accept credit cards in our store. Luckily, this is where the Payment Service Providers jump in. These are third-party companies handling the payment transactions for you in a secure way. Simplify Commerce that we just mentioned, is just one of the many options you have. However, your country of residence will influence the number of possibilities you can choose from.

Just by checking out the WooCommerce extensions page, you'll get an idea of what's possible for your market: `http://www.woothemes.com/product-category/woocommerce-extensions/`.

Select Payment Gateways and your country to receive an overview of available, payment extensions for WooCommerce:

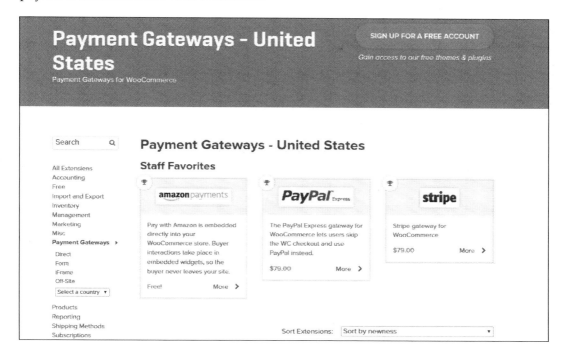

The extensions to support Payment Service Providers aren't free at the WooThemes website. Sometimes the Payment Service Provider of your choice might offer a free extension for WooCommerce when you sign up. Just make sure that you check if it is available. Installing an extension works in the same way as with any regular WordPress plugin. After installing the plugin there's always some configuration that needs to be done. The steps you need to take differ per Payment Gateway.

The extensions at the WooThemes website can sometimes be pricey. But you will receive support and updates for a year, which can be a good reason still to choose for a WooThemes plugin. Alternatively, there are lots of WooCommerce compatible extensions offered at the CodeCanyon website: `http://codecanyon.net/ category/wordpress/ecommerce/woocommerce`. The quality of these plugins may differ, so please pay attention to the ratings and comments of other users.

It's wise to take some time to find the right Payment Service Provider for your market. Pay attention to the rates charged by the Payment Service Provider (as well transaction fees as monthly rates) and the way they will pay you after the transaction.

Setting up a contract with a Payment Service Provider of your choice and the way the setup is done in WooCommerce differs a lot. Therefore, in our example below, we've chosen to just stick to the default options of WooCommerce.

Setting up PayPal

Setting up PayPal in your WooCommerce store is very simple. Of course you first need to create a PayPal account if you do not yet have one at `http://www.paypal.com`. Mark it as a business account and enter your bank account details to be able to transfer money from your PayPal account to your regular bank account.

Next, in WooCommerce, click **PayPal** at the top of the **Payment Gateways** tab

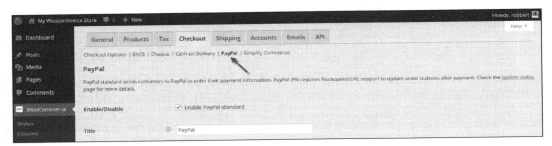

Enter the e-mail address that you used to create your PayPal account:

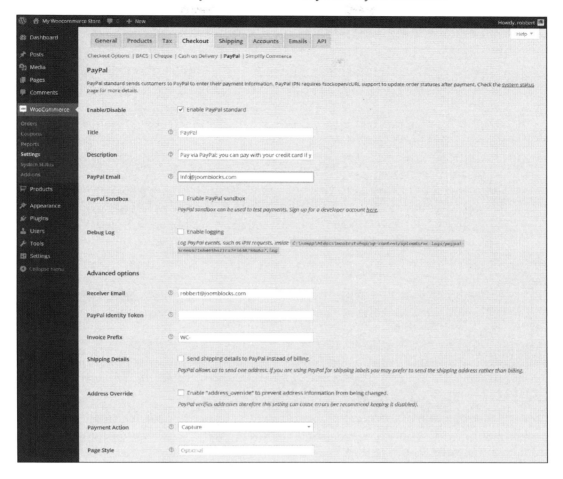

Note that you have the following possibilities:

- You can use a PayPal Sandbox function, to test your transactions, before your store is opened for customers. For more information about the Sandbox functions of PayPal, see `https://developer.paypal.com/`. When testing, you can also enable **the Debug Log** to receive detailed information about your transaction. Generally, you don't need this, the plugin should work out of the box.

- Use an **Invoice prefix**, that is used to create the transaction number. By default, this is WC (from WooCommerce), so you might want to use something different. Note that the invoice number will be sent to PayPal including the prefix. If you would be running multiple WooCommerce stores using one PayPal account, you need to use a different prefix for every store.

- Use Page styles, defined within your PayPal account, to be able to offer a non-standard look and feel of the PayPal checkout page. More information about using Page styles can be found here: `https://www.paypal.com/customize`.

 Note: regardless of the Payment Service Gateway you're using, make sure that you test your setup thoroughly. Don't hesitate to buy and pay for a product in your own store. It's important that you've actually checked the process completely, instead of assuming that it will work!

Setting up Stripe

Stripe is a payment method created for software developers. Meanwhile the service became more mature and is now available in more than 20 countries, among which the USA, Australia, and a part of Western Europe.

To be able to use Stripe, your website must use a SSL certificate. Without it, you cannot use Stripe in a production environment. If you'd like to receive more information on SSL: your hosting provider can help you. A good option could be Namecheap (`https://www.namecheap.com/security/ssl-certificates.aspx`), which has a pretty good acceptance and is very affordable. Even better, but also more expensive is Digicert (`https://www.digicert.com/buy-ssl-certificates.htm`). Note that Digicert also offers a lot of information on using SSL certificates.

After signing up for a Stripe account (`http://stripe.com`), you just have to confirm your e-mail address to get started. For WooCommerce, there are a couple of options. There's a plugin available at WooThemeshere: `http://www.woothemes.com/products/stripe/`.

There's also a free extension available through the WordPress.org website (`https://wordpress.org/plugins/stripe-for-woocommerce/`). And that's the one we'll be using in our example below:

- First install the Stripe plugin for WooCommerce by uploading it to your WordPress installation or just download and install it directly from WordPress.

- After activating the plugin navigate to **WooCommerce | Settings | Checkout**.

- Copy your API keys from the Stripe website (`https://dashboard.stripe.com/account/apikeys`) and paste them into your settings page:

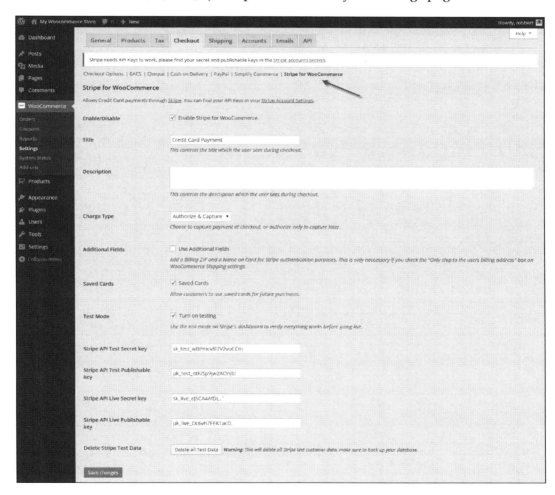

- Enable **Turn on testing,** so that you can start with testing Stripe Credit card payments in your store.

That's all you need to setup a working solution to accept credit cards on your website. The exact procedure for other payment gateways will differ, but generally the steps will look similar.

 The mentioned, free plugin for working with Stripe currently doesn't work very well together with the Subscriptions plugin. If you need to sell subscriptions this plugin is not the best choice at moment of writing. More on working with subscriptions will follow in *Chapter 8, More Possibilities Using Plugins*.

For the other, offline Payment Methods, it's just a matter of enabling or disabling them as you please. You are able to change the description that your visitors will see for every payment method. The Cash on Delivery payment method also gives the possibility to connect it to a shipping method. That's useful so you'll be able to set a different price for using this method, since Cash on Delivery is often an expensive choice.

Shipping methods and prices

Just as with Payment Methods, we also need to think about the shipping methods we are going to offer to our customers. Where are we going to ship to? Do we charge our customers for it and if yes, does the amount depend on the shipping address, the weight of the products or both? Also in here we have to think about several aspects:

- Which carrier(s) are we going to use?
- Is there any integration needed of our orders with that carrier or will we work manually?
- What are our shipping prices and in which way are we going to calculate shipping to our customers?

Looking at the functions WooCommerce is offering we see a similar screen as used for Payment Methods. There are a couple of settings that we need to check:

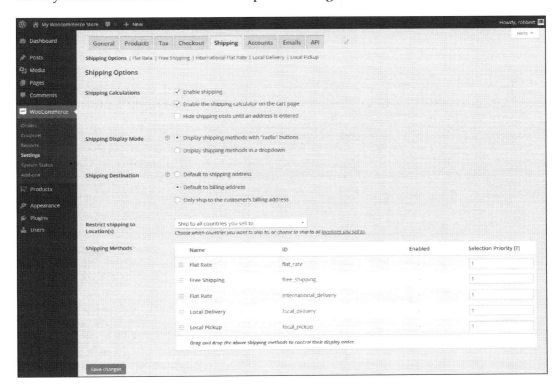

At the top of the screen we'll find all settings regarding shipping, which we already discussed during *Chapter 1, Setting Up WooCommerce*.

Below the settings we'll find all standard available shipping methods. Every Shipping Method has a link on top of the screen that will bring us to the settings page for that Shipping Method. This is what WooCommerce has to offer by default:

- **Flat Rate**, a fixed amount of shipping costs for all orders.
- **Free Shipping**, speaks for itself.
- **International Delivery**, for customers outside of our own country. Similar to Flat Rate shipping. The amount does not differ per country.
- **Local Delivery**, for customers living near us. We could enter zip codes to specify when this method will be available.

You may sort the table by dragging the various shipping methods around. This is useful because the sorting here will also be the sort order of shipping methods the user sees during checkout. Besides that, using the priority field you can control the order in which the shipping methods are selected. If two or more Shipping Methods have the same priority, the one with the lowest cost will be selected first.

- **Local Pickup**. Instead of delivering the order, our customers could also pick it up of course. WooCommerce assumes that in this case there's no charge for our customer.

Let's take a closer look at the **Flat Rate** method, just to check how we need to configure it. Just click on the **Flat Rate** link at the top of your screen. The **Flat Rate** method will calculate one shipping rate per order, regardless of the weight and dimensions of the products in that order. The **Flat Rate** cannot differ per country, but the field **Costs** can contain a calculation, which means that the **Flat Rate** can also be a percentage of the total order value:

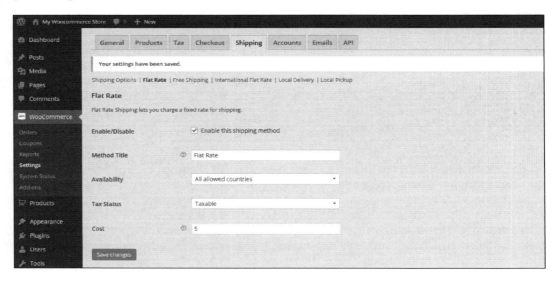

Some examples of a calculated **Cost** field could be:

- **5 + (1 * [qty])** Which would calculate $5 for every order plus $1 extra for every item in that order
- **10 + [fee percent="10″ min_fee="2″]** Would calculate a base amount of $10 plus 10% of the order total with a minimum of $2

Looking at the available Shipping Methods, we can imagine running short on possibilities. What if we need a Shipping Method that calculates the shipping rate based on the country, delivery address and the products that we'll ship? That's no longer a Flat Rate anymore and the other shipping methods do not offer a solution. In such a situation, WooCommerce needs additional extensions. A good and very flexible, but pretty expensive extension would be the Table Rate shipping plugin. It's available for $199 at the WooCommerce store: `http://www.woothemes.com/products/table-rate-shipping-2/`.

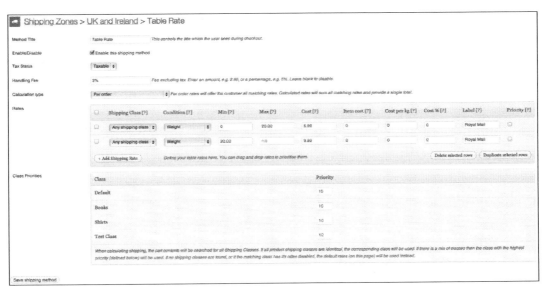

Because of the higher price of the official WooThemes extension, there's room for alternative suppliers in the market. On CodeCanyon, there's a reasonably priced plugin available. `http://codecanyon.net/item/table-rate-shipping-for-woocommerce/3796656`. It's already been on the market for a while now and has a lot of users.

Working with free shipping

Nowadays buyers often expect to receive free shipping when ordering items in your store. Shipping costs that are too high can be a reason for customers to leave your store and look for an alternative. WooCommerce offers a shipping method that gives the possibility to ship items for free. Let's have a look at the options:

- As with the other Shipping Methods, you must enable **Free Shipping** to be able to use it.

- Next, determine which countries you want to offer free shipping to, using the **field Method availability**:

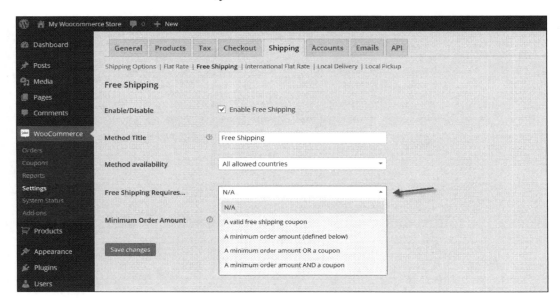

- Choose if there are any requirements that must be met before offering free shipping. You have the choice to set this to the following options:
    - **A valid free shipping coupon**. We'll see coupon creation later on in this chapter.
    - **A minimum order amount**. If you choose this one, also set the value in the field below: **Minimum Order Amount**.
    - A combination of these two, where you have the possibility to choose OR and AND. In case of OR just one of the two requirements needs to be met to receive free shipping. In case of AND both requirements must be met to receive free shipping.

Using shipping classes

You must have noticed earlier in this book when creating products that there's a field named **Shipping class** that can be assigned to your products. A shipping class is nothing more than a connection between a product and a certain way of shipping. In other words, a shipping class can be assigned to a product. If we define multiple shipping classes, it becomes easier to use different shipping rates for different types of products. Defining shipping classes is just as easy as creating new categories. Just navigate in your WordPress menu on the left to **Products | Shipping classes**. Just enter a **Name** and **Description** for your class and click the button **Add New Shipping Class**:

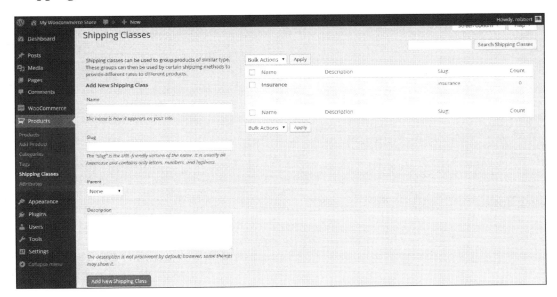

Once done, it's possible to set a rate per shipping class. Whether or not it is possible to set a rate per shipping class also depends on the shipping method. This way of working could be helpful when, for example, you're selling items of a higher value that need additional insurance:

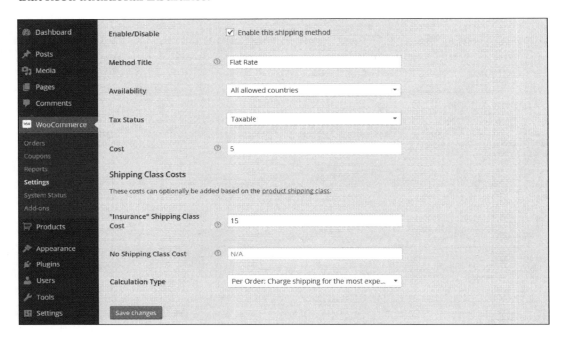

In this example we see that, when an item is part of the shipping class Insurance, there's a cost of $20 for shipping ($5 + $15), instead of the regular $5. The **Calculation Type** makes sure that the higher cost is only calculated once for the complete order. It's also possible to calculate the additional fee for every item on the order having this specific shipping class.

Carrier integration

As with Payment Methods, there are lots of carriers on the market that offer integration with WooCommerce, so that you will not have to handle shipping transactions manually. There are too many possibilities to mention here, but there's always an extension needed to connect WooCommerce to a specific carrier.

If you're in need of integrating a carrier, head back to the WooCommerce website to check if there's an extension available: `http://www.woothemes.com/product-category/woocommerce-extensions/`. For major player like UPS and FedEx, extensions are available, but these extensions will only calculate the correct shipping rates for these carriers.

Using discount coupons

There's one more topic we would like to discuss in this chapter. Working with discount coupons gives you the possibility to organize promotions for your existing customers, subscribers, or any other target group. WooCommerce has the basic functionality on board to be able to work with discount coupons. You may find them in the menu by navigating to **WooCommerce | Coupons**:

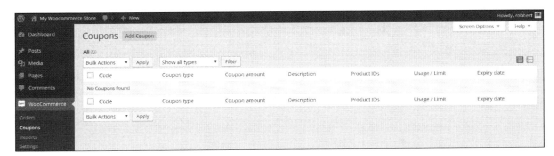

To add a new coupon, click on the **Add Coupon** button at the top of the screen:

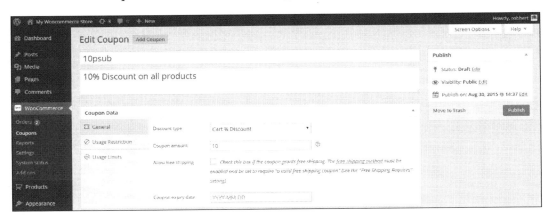

In the preceding example above we created a simple coupon that gives a 10% discount on the whole cart. To enable our coupon, we now simply need to hit the **Publish** button.

The Coupon function delivers several possibilities; let's go through the fields one by one:

- First of all, set the coupon code at the top of the screen. This is the code that your customers need to enter to be able to receive the discount. Keep it short.

- Next, enter a description for your coupon so that you will recognize it later on.

- An important one is **Discount type**. You may choose to give a discount as a fixed amount per product, as a percentage of the sale price per product, as a fixed amount for the whole cart or as a percentage for the whole cart. We used this last one, the setting **Cart % Discount**.

- Below the type field, set the amount or percentage of discount you want to give in the **Coupon amount** field.

- Besides the mentioned possibilities for giving an amount or percentage of discount, it's also possible to offer free shipping to your customers using a coupon. Check **Allow free shipping** if you want to use this function. However, note that it's also needed to enable the Free Shipping method we saw earlier and set it so that a coupon must be used.

- Next, we can also enter a **Coupon Expiry** date, so that when that date is reached, the coupon will no longer work.

- Other options can be found by clicking on the tabs on the left named **Usage Restriction** and **Usage Limits**:

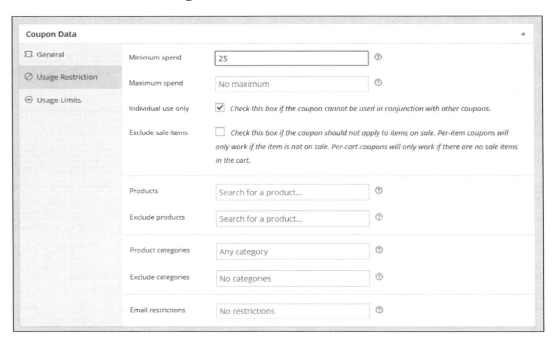

- You may restrict the coupon by entering a **Minimum spend** and/or **Maximum spend**, so that discount is only given to orders that meet these rules. Handy if you want to run a promotion like Receive 20% discount on all orders of $100 and over.

- Check the **Individual use only** field if you want to prevent your customers from combining several coupon codes.

- Can your customers use the coupon to buy items that are already on sale? If not, check the **Exclude sale items** field.

- Next, we can limit our coupon code to certain products or categories, or even exclude certain products or categories from the promotion. Just choose whatever is most convenient in your situation. Note: you cannot mix these rules. For example, if you exclude a certain category, you cannot include a specific product in the same category. There would be a conflict between the two rules, which will not work.

- Use the **Email restrictions** field if you want to make this field available only to some specific customer(s). You must know the e-mail address they will use to place their order to be able to use this. WooCommerce uses the e-mail address entered in the checkout form for this restriction. That doesn't have to be the same one as the e-mail address on the customer's account.

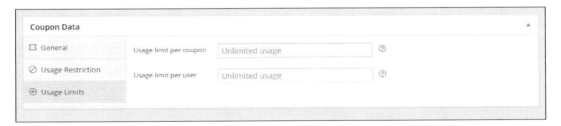

- Finally, there are two more settings to limit the usage of our coupon. First, we can set how many times this coupon may be used. Note that the **Usage limit per coupon** setting works on store level, this won't stop a specific customer to use the same coupon code multiple times for different orders. If you want to prevent that from happening, use the **Usage limit per user** setting.

At the **Cart** or **Checkout**, your customers will be asked to enter a coupon if they
have one:

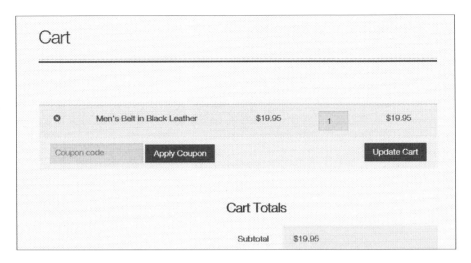

Note that the way this looks like completely depends on the theme you're using.
Be aware that as soon as you enable the usage of coupons, potential customers that
do not have one might be distracted and leave the cart to start searching for one.
Sometimes it's just better to keep the function disabled, if you're not running any
promotions where coupons are needed.

Once your customer applies the coupon to the order, the order review section looks
as follows:

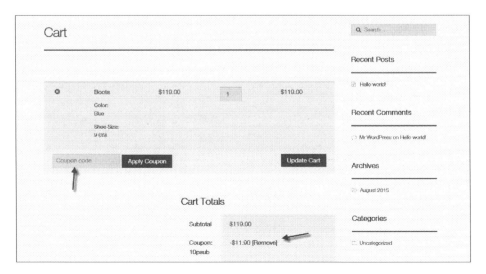

After adding the coupon, your customer can delete the coupon code again by clicking the **Remove** link.

Depending on the settings of your coupons, it will be allowed or disallowed to use multiple coupons for the same order.

Summary

During this chapter we've learned to work with the default Payment possibilities WooCommerce is offering. However, every country is different and it's important that you use the right payment solution for your area. We've also learned how to use the functions WooCommerce offers to calculate shipping costs. Finally, we've worked with discount coupons, to be used for marketing purposes.

In the next chapter we are going to change the look and feel of our store. We'll have a closer look at WordPress themes, tailored to work with WooCommerce.

5
Working with WooCommerce Themes

So far we've been able to setup our online store, add different type of products and take the necessary steps to add payment and shipping methods. We already installed the free Storefront theme earlier, but our shop still looks very standard though. It's time to change the look and feel of our store!

In this chapter we'll cover:

- Using the available widgets and shortcodes
- Making or buying a theme
- Finding and selecting WooCommerce themes
- Using the free Storefront theme
- Changing the Storefront theme using the customizer

Using the available widgets and shortcodes

When you installed WooCommerce, you also received a number of possibilities that you can use to show products to your visitors. Of course there are the default available shop, category and product pages. But sometimes, you need more than that. Let's look at the other options that WooCommerce offers by default.

WooCommerce offers the following widgets, that you can reach from the Theme customizer or via **Appearance | Widgets**:

- **WooCommerce Layered Nav Filters**
- **WooCommerce Price filter**
- **WooCommerce Product Categories**
- **WooCommerce Products**
- **WooCommerce Product Search**
- **WooCommerce Product Tags**
- **WooCommerce Recently Viewed**
- **WooCommerce Recent Review**
- **WooCommerce Top Rated Products**

The screenshot is as follows:

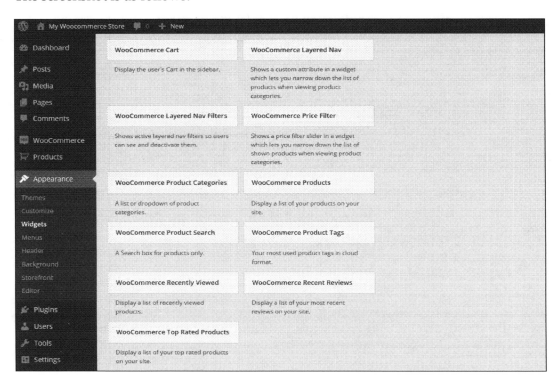

Using these widgets is easy and works just like any other WordPress widget. Using a couple of these in your sidebar gives your visitors the flexibility they need to find their way in your store. In the example below you see we activated the following widgets: **WooCommerce Product Search, WooCommerce Products** and **WooCommerce Product Categories**:

Note that the sidebar is on the right in this example. Generally it makes more sense in an online store to have such a sidebar on the left. This is something you can just set in the Storefront theme. Later on in this chapter we'll give you more information on customizing the Storefront theme.

Making or buying a theme

The look and feel of your store is completely controlled by your WordPress theme. We already noticed that even a theme like Storefront already delivers good results. It's just better to use a theme that has been created with using WooCommerce in mind. If you would use a standard WordPress theme like Twenty Fifteen or Twenty Sixteen WooCommerce will still work, but layout issues might occur.

We have two possibilities when choosing a design for our store:

- Design and develop a theme from scratch. Or have someone do that for us
- Use a WooCommerce theme that is available on the market

To start with the first option, creating a theme ourselves is not something we could do overnight. It requires extensive knowledge of Web design, WordPress, WooCommerce, PHP, HTML, and CSS, Just to name a few. But maybe, if we wanted to have a unique design that no other shop is using, this could still be a good choice. It just requires more time and a large budget to do so. Creating your own WordPress or WooCommerce theme is a learning experience if you never did it before.

The alternative is using a standard theme. These are themes optimized for WooCommerce and available out of the box. Using a standard theme you can start right away. Some of them are even free, like for instance the good Storefront theme. We'll often find that we need a commercial theme though. Commercial or Premium themes can be found in price ranges from $20 to $200, where the majority of the themes will be offered below $100. If we had a small budget this would definitely be the way to go, since there are hundreds of themes to choose from. Remember that it's always possible to make adjustments on these themes, so that the theme of your choice better fits your needs.

Finding and selecting WooCommerce themes

If you decided to use a standard theme you'll face a new challenge: which theme will fit your needs? There are free themes available on the market, but most WooCommerce themes are commercial themes you'll have to pay for. Often they are referred to as Premium themes. These themes are supported by the developer and deliver lots of functions in most cases. That's not always a good thing though. Functionality should be provided by plugins and not within the theme itself. Besides that, having too much functions will just slow down your website. As a beginner this is sometimes difficult to judge. Just pick what you really need and do not go for the theme that offers the most functions. Look for themes that make it easy to customize the layout, colors and fonts. There are a number of resources available online to look for WooCommerce-compatible themes:

- The WooThemes website (http://www.woothemes.com) from the developers of WooCommerce. In fact, WooThemes exists much longer than their WooCommerce product, which is relatively young. Look at the demos to check how category and product pages will look like. The good thing of a theme created by WooThemes is that it will be an absolutely quality theme and compatible with WooCommerce. Themes found on WooThemes are not the cheapest ones. Pricing starts at around $80. Pay attention to the child themes. They have a low price, but also require the theme that it was built on. The following image shows a screenshot of Outlet, one of the available themes at WooThemes.com:

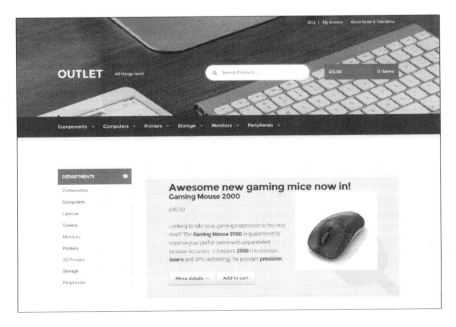

- **ThemeForest** at `http://themeforest.net/category/wordpress/ecommerce/woocommerce`. ThemeForest is a marketplace, where lots of developers are offering themes for WordPress and other solutions. There's a large range of WooCommerce enabled themes available. But please note that the quality may differ. Carefully look at the demos, the comments of other readers, and the last time that it was updated. Reasonably priced themes are around $60.

  The image below shows the Integrity theme demo created using the X-theme, one of the many versatile and flexible WooCommerce themes at ThemeForest.com:

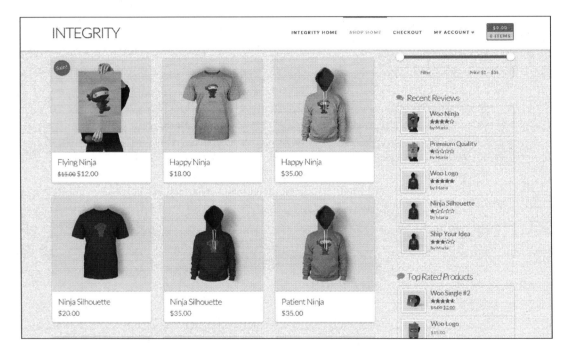

- Even cheaper themes can be found elsewhere on the Internet For instance at Elegantthemes (`http://www.elegantthemes.com/gallery/`) or Mojo Themes (`http://www.mojo-themes.com/categories/wordpress/ecommerce-wordpress/woocommerce-themes/`).

Sometimes, you may find free themes as well. The best resources are WooThemes and the WordPress.org website: `http://wordpress.org/themes/`. Search for WooCommerce if you're searching on WordPress.org. All themes can be used, but using a theme built for WooCommerce often gives better results out of the box. Be careful building your business on a free theme. Although it seems tempting if you're on a low budget, free themes are often not updated or supported. If there's any free theme we can really recommend, then it would be the Storefront theme, that is also used in this book. It is well written, and a good starting point if you want to learn WooCommerce theme development yourself. It is supported by WooThemes as well, which is an important asset for a free theme.

I also wrote a roundup of free WooCommerce themes on my blog. If you need to limit yourself to free themes, you should check it out. You may find it here:

`http://www.joomblocks.com/best-free-woocommerce-themes-2015.`

Things you should pay attention to when buying a theme

If you're not yet very familiar with working with different WordPress themes, then the following guidelines may be helpful to come to a good choice:

- Browser compatibility: For users, this isn't always clear, but often older browsers like Microsoft Internet Explorer 8 and older are no longer supported. This means that a visitor using such a browser will see a malfunctioning website. Depending on your audience, this is or isn't a problem. Just pay attention to it and make sure that you understand on which browsers and versions the theme of your choice will work.

- Smartphone/Tablet compatibility: Nowadays, when building a website, you have to consider how your site will look on mobile devices. Meet this requirement by looking for a Responsive WooCommerce theme. A website built with a responsive theme will look good on all devices, independent of their maximum screen resolution. Themes that are also Retina ready will look good on high resolution screens like the latest iPad 3 as well. See the example below of a responsive theme and how the look and feel will change if the website is visited using a mobile phone (on the right-hand side):

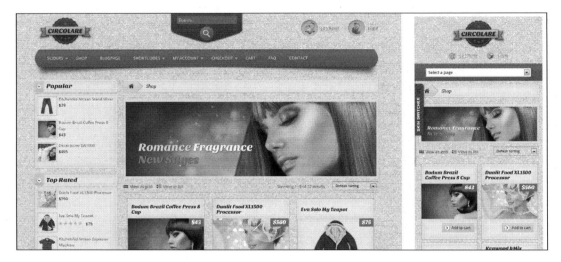

 Theme developers almost always offer a demo site where you can check how the theme looks like. Don't forget to open this demo page with a tablet and mobile phone as well to get an idea of the layout on those devices.

- Is the theme compatible with the latest version of WooCommerce? Check the current version of the WooCommerce plugin and check if the theme developer guarantees that it will work. Also here, when buying a theme from WooThemes, there should be no incompatibility issues.

- When was the theme updated? Especially when buying from third party developers like on the ThemeForest marketplace, it's important to check if the developer is keeping the theme up to date. Having an updated theme is important. An older theme might not be compatible anymore with the latest WordPress and WooCommerce versions.

- How flexible is the theme from the functional point of view? For example, will you be able to easily change colors? Can you change the layout of the theme a bit without coding? Is there enough space in the header for your logo?

- What other functions are being delivered? Also important: do you really need all the functions that are being delivered in the theme? We often see themes with tons of functionality. Using such functions is handy, but your website might break if you're ever going to switch to a different theme. For example, we nowadays, regularly see themes with built-in functions for **Search Engine Optimization (SEO)**. If you would switch themes in the future, you might even lose such data! Even if the theme offers functionality like this, it's better to take advantage of a separate SEO plugin. This will prevent the loss of data if you ever want to change to a different theme in the future.

There are a lot of things that we have to pay attention to when buying a WooCommerce theme. However, when creating a theme from scratch, we need to pay attention to some of these topics as well. In this case, we must have, or gather, the knowledge to be able to build it correctly.

Installing a WooCommerce theme

If you bought a commercial WooCommerce-compatible theme, you will have to install it through the WordPress administrative panel or upload it using FTP. Before we do so, let's first take a look at what we actually received. In almost all cases, you'll receive a ZIP file holding different folders. The content and names of the folders will differ from theme to theme. Still, it's good to have a closer look at it and get familiar with commercial theme packages.

An example of the contents of a downloaded theme can be found in the next screenshot:

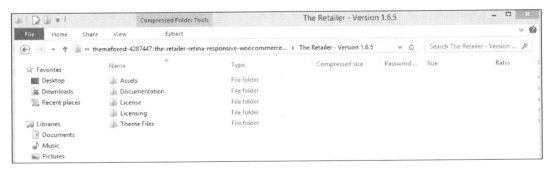

Note that this is just an example, coming from a ThemeForest WooCommerce theme named The Retailer. The folder structure of this theme shows that it differs from just a regular WordPress theme. There are separate folders holding `Assets`, the original Photoshop files and Demo data for instance. The actual theme files we need to install the theme have been placed in the folder theme files and we first need to extract (unzip) the whole package in order to be able to continue with our installation. Although the folder names will differ from theme to theme, this is an approach that you will see with lots of premium themes. Always look for a folder named `Documentation` and start reading this before doing anything else! Often, you'll see that the documentation is offered in an HTML format, starting with `index.html` that you should open using your browser. In the following screenshot, there's an example of such a documentation:

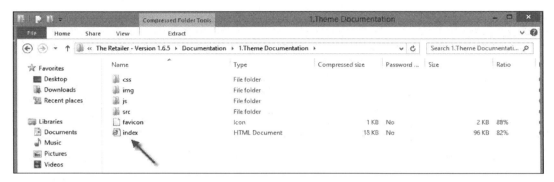

To install the theme, we head over to the WordPress administrator and choose **Appearance | Themes** in the menu. Click on **Add New**, and then click on the **Upload Theme** link:

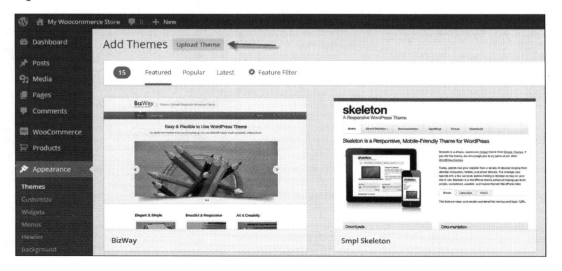

Click on **Choose file**, and then browse to the folder where you unpacked the theme files a minute ago. We open the file `theretailer.zip` from the subfolder named `Theme files` and click on **Install Now**. Remember to upload the ZIP file and not the theme folder inside it.

Next, since this theme is already delivering a child theme, we'll install that one as well. We repeat the preceding steps for the file `theretailer-child.zip`. Note that we must do it in this order: first install the main or parent theme and after that the child theme. Besides that not every theme will deliver a child theme as well. Often, you'll just receive a single theme package.

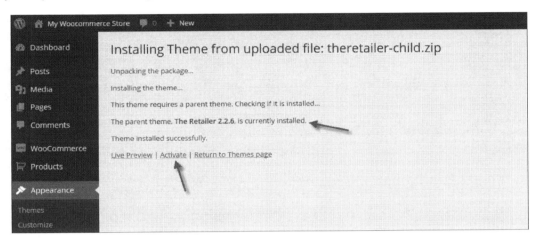

Working with Child theme is a best practice if you need to make changes to your theme. By using a parent and child theme, we'll avoid losing our changes if the developer ever needs to update the theme—and this will happen. If the theme of your choice does not deliver a child theme in the package, it's not very difficult to create one. More on child themes will follow in *Chapter 6, Customizing a WooCommerce Theme*.

Don't forget to activate the Child theme by clicking on the link after installation!
Note that our theme requires us to install a couple of additional plugins. We receive
a warning message that we can do this by clicking on the link, as shown in the
following screenshot:

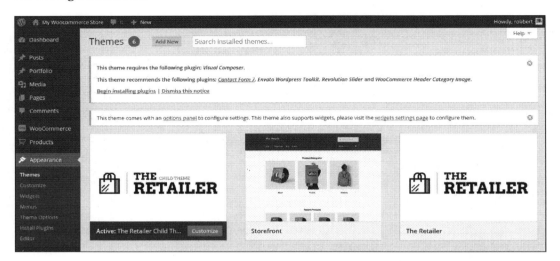

You would see the following screen after clicking on the link:

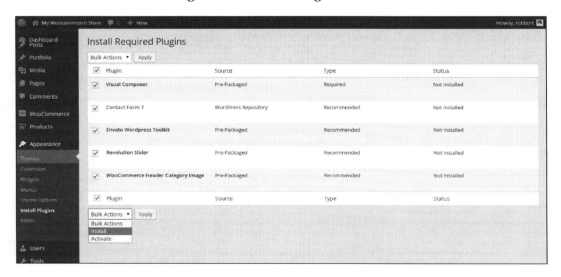

Select the plugins and install them all at the same time.

Whether or not your theme will ask for similar steps completely depends on the way it was set up by the developer. Refer to the documentation for your theme when you're in doubt about the steps to take. Note that after bulk-installing the plugins, we also need to activate them.

 Premium themes are regularly delivered including demo content. If you are a beginner and find it difficult to start, it's often a good idea to install the demo content in your WordPress test environment. By combining the theme and demo content, is just gets easier to know the theme and its functions. Use the WordPress importer (**Tools | Import** in the menu) to import the demo content.

After installing the parent and child themes and activating it, our store page looks as follows on the frontend:

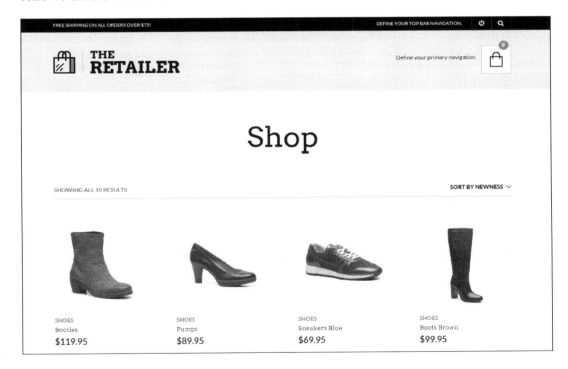

It's functional but still requires additional setup.

Working with theme settings

WordPress is expanding the standard functions to work with theme settings since WordPress version 3.4. However, we can see that the possibilities have been too limited for premium themes and developers continued to work with their own solutions. This is changing though and WordPress puts in more and more effort on customizing your theme using the default WordPress customizer. In this example, the theme comes with its own solution. We can find the settings of our theme by navigating to **Appearance | Theme** options, but you might just as well find a new high-level menu item for your theme. The following screenshot shows the options for our theme:

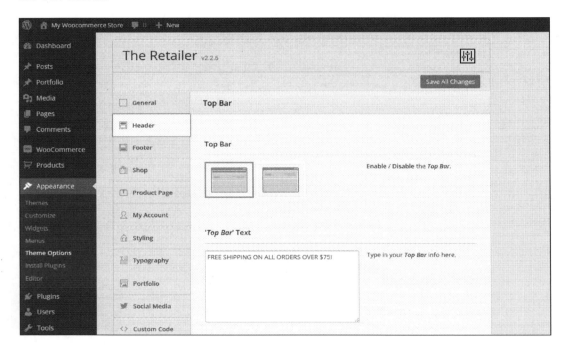

Our theme, The Retailer, offers an extended option panel with lots of options to set up our store and change the look and feel. Of course, we can upload our own logo, but it's also possible to change colors, fonts, the contents of the header and footer, and many more. There's no use in exploring all the possibilities here because they are theme-specific. Your situation will be different depending on the theme that you're using.

In the remaining part of this book, we'll switch back to the free Storefront theme. It gives us possibilities to show theme customization and development examples in a better way.

 Do you like the way the theme, The Retailer, looks like and its flexibility to change all the colors just the way you need them? The theme is available for purchase at http://themeforest.net/item/the-retailer-retina-responsive-woocommerce-theme/4287447.

Setting up your home page

There's one more item that we need to discuss that is generic and not really dependent on the theme you're using. Although it is a basic WordPress setting, we still see lots of users getting confused about it. When you have just installed WordPress, by default it will always show blog items on the Front page. For an online store that isn't suitable. You want to show products, maybe a slider and some other information. But in most cases not the blog. If you don't know how to change that here' how:

1. First, navigate to **Pages** and create a new page named Homepage. Do not fill any content, just publish it. Note that sometimes, you'll have to set the page template to home page or front page, depending on your theme. Refer to your theme documentation if you're not sure.

2. Repeat this step and create a page named Blog.

3. Head over to the WordPress **Settings** menu and click on **Reading**. In here, change the **Front page displays** to **A static page** and select the pages that you just created. The following screenshot shows an example. Save your settings and you're done. Depending on the way your theme works, it will automatically start filling your home page with a slider, products, or other items. Please refer to your theme documentation for more information.

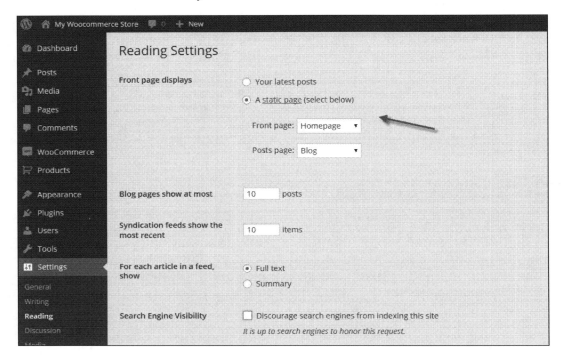

Using the Storefront theme

The Storefront theme is definitely one of the better free themes. That makes sense because it was developed by the creators of WooCommerce.

The functionality of Storefront is a bit limited. However, you can expand the functionality by installing additional plugins for Storefront, which you have to pay for. Let's first take a look at the changes that you can make by default.

After activating the theme, it will add additional menu items to the **Appearance** menu in WordPress. Here, you'll find several shortcuts for additional possibilities. WooThemes is a commercial company after all, so there are plenty of links here for more options, which you have to pay for.

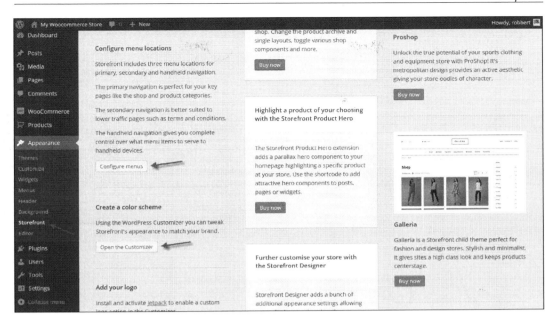

Whether you click on the link to **Configure menus** or **Open the Customizer**, in both cases the WordPress customizer will be opened. Since WordPress 4.3, you can change your menus from within the customizer, but the old function using **Appearance | Menus** is still available:

Just navigate the various options to change the items that you need, for example, the background and font colors.

Note that the **Layout** option on the left gives the possibility to show the sidebar on the left, which makes sense for a typical online store.

Adding a logo

It's possible to add a header image to the Storefront theme. But strangely enough, Storefront does not offer the possibility to add your company logo, and the header image isn't really meant for this. To solve this problem, you must download and install the Storefront Logo Plugin, which will add the function to the customizer, at `https://wordpress.org/plugins/storefront-site-logo/`. Alternatively, you may also use the WordPress Jetpack plugin, which also gives you the possibility to change the logo `http://jetpack.me/`.

Homepage control

Another plugin that you really want to install when working with the Storefront theme is Homepage control. Use it if you decide to use a regular page as a home page for your website instead of the blog. Download it at `https://wordpress.org/plugins/homepage-control/`. Once activated, navigate to the customizer again to switch off any area that you do not want to include on your homepage:

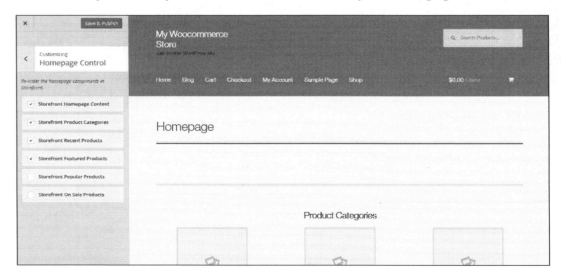

Did you notice that Storefront also shows an image for your product categories on the home page? You can switch these off, but if you want to keep them, navigate to **Products | Categories** and add an image for every category.

Let's have a look at our current result using the Storefront theme and without changing a single line of code!

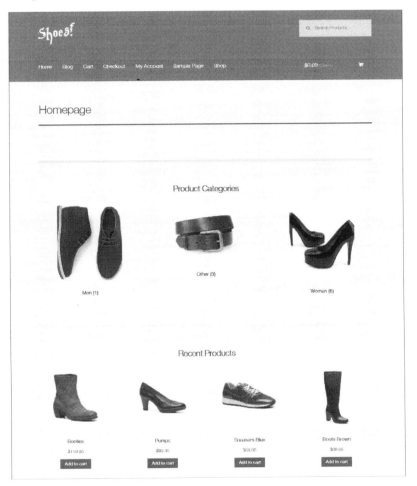

You might want to make more changes to the theme, but changing code is something that we'll discuss in the next chapter. Before we dive into code, please also have a look at the Storefront customization plugin. It's not free, but gives you additional possibilities to change the look and feel of your store (http://www.woothemes.com/products/storefront-woocommerce-customiser/).

Summary

There are lots of WooCommerce-compatible themes on the market. We've seen that working with a theme isn't difficult as long as you take the time to read the documentation and get to know your theme. The exact way of working may differ from theme to theme though, especially for premium themes.

The Storefront theme is giving us a good and solid base, and even without changing code, we can already reach a good-looking result.

In the next chapter, we'll have a closer look at the ability to modify the code of the Storefront theme.

6

Customizing a WooCommerce Theme

Working with standard themes is a quick and effective solution to get your store up and running, but soon you'll feel the need to make changes to the theme that you're using. Or leave the standard theme and create one from scratch yourself. In this book, I cannot offer you a complete development course. I'll discuss the basics that will give you a good start, working with the Storefront theme. In this chapter, we will cover:

- General directions for changing or creating a WordPress theme
- Tips for changing or creating a WooCommerce theme
- Some practical examples of changes in the Storefront theme

What we need to get started

First of all, before we do anything at all, you need to be aware of the fact that this chapter is not suitable for the real beginners. Did you ever work with HTML, CSS, and PHP and have some experience in these areas? Good, then you're good to move forward. If you do not yet have knowledge on these topics, it's probably better to skip this chapter and jump to *Chapter 7, Running Your Online Store*. That will be easier to follow.

If you're not yet familiar with the techniques mentioned, there's plenty of information available on the Internet to get you started. From short tutorials to complete online video training, everything is already there. The following websites are highly recommended:

- The Tuts+ network from Envato: For instance `http://webdesign. tutsplus.com/` and `http://wp.tutsplus.com/`. The Tuts+ network also offers additional tutorials and video training as a paid service.
- Smashing Magazine: at `http://www.smashingmagazine.com/`. Besides their web design tutorials and special WordPress corner available at `http:// wp.smashingmagazine.com/`, they also offer a recommended book series.

Would you rather work directly from a book? In that case, we can recommend the following books from Packt Publishing:

- Responsive Web Design by Example : Beginner's Guide: `https://www. packtpub.com/web-development/responsive-web-design-example`
- Responsive Web Design with HTML5 and CSS3: `https://www.packtpub. com/web-development/responsive-web-design-html5-and-css3`
- WordPress Theme Development : Beginner's guide - Third Edition: `https:// www.packtpub.com/web-development/wordpress-theme-development- beginners-guide`

This chapter is too short to cover the topic of WordPress theme development completely. As we've seen, there have been complete books written about these topics. For this chapter, we'll stick to the basics and add specific WooCommerce information on top of that.

Before you start making changes to your theme, find out if it's really necessary to do so. WooCommerce comes with a lot of shortcodes that you can easily use on your posts and pages to call WooCommerce functions that you need. See `http://docs. woothemes.com/document/woocommerce-shortcodes/` for a full list and examples.

Tools every web designer needs

Every web designer or developer has his/her own favorite tools. That's fine; just use what you like. If you're just starting, the minimum that you need is as follows:

- An image editor. Photoshop is top-notch, but expensive. Photoshop elements would work as well, just as the free, open source Gimp.

- A plain text editor, being able to help you with your HTML, CSS, and PHP files. Windows users could look at the free Notepad++, Coda is a good tool for Mac users but has its price. Alternatively, have a look at Sublime Text, which has a free version.

- A set of browsers and devices to test your work. Do not underestimate this part, it could be very annoying and time-consuming to fix some issues that are related to a specific browser and version. Firefox users should look at the Firebug plugin as well, it really helps when making changes on a theme to be able to see them immediately. Chrome and Safari have such functions built-in. The example below shows Google Chrome. Using the Inspect element function (just right-click on any element on your page), you are able to see which CSS styles were applied to that element. You may easily try to change the CSS code, but please note that these changes will not be stored and are only useful to test them. The following image below shows you the Inspect element function within Chrome:

WordPress theme basics

WordPress theme development in a short version:

- Every WordPress theme has its own folder, which you may find in the `wp-content/themes` folder of your WordPress installation.

- The bare minimum that every WordPress theme needs is an `index.php` and `style.css` file. The `index.php` file determines the way the home page looks like, by the so-called WordPress loop. There are also other possibilities for the home page, which we'll see in a minute. The `style.css` file contains all the styling or calls for other CSS files. It also contains the name and author of the theme.

- From `index.php`, lots of different PHP files can be called. Here are a couple of the most common ones, including their meaning:

  - `header.php`: This contains the logic for the header of your theme, which mostly contains things such as the logo, website name, search bar, and menu. It also contains the necessary HTML head code.

  - `sidebar.php`: This contains the definition of a sidebar, that is used to display widgets. More complex themes often give the possibility to use multiple sidebars with different content.

  - `footer.php`: This contains some closing tags for the theme. Besides that, it has become quite common to define additional widget areas in the footer as well.

  - `home.php`: This file can be used to show the latest blog posts on the landing page for your blog. Often, this is the home page of your website, but it doesn't have to be. If WordPress is set up to use a static page as the home page, then `home.php` could be used for your blog.

  - `front-page.php`: If this file exists, it will be used for the home page of the website. If it doesn't exist, WordPress will look for `home.php`. If both of them don't exist, `index.php` will be used. For a deeper explanation, have a look at `http://codex.wordpress.org/Creating_a_Static_Front_Page`.

- ° `single.php`: This is used to display a single post type—often, a single blog item.

- ° `page.php`: This is used to display a single WordPress page.

- ° `functions.php`: This is an important one because, here, you'll define all kinds of different functions for your theme, for instance, the widget positions, theme support for post thumbnails, and so on. Also, when creating WooCommerce themes, `functions.php` plays an important role. Using `functions.php`, you are able to add features and functions to your website. Note that for larger changes, creating a plugin is a better option though.

Are you making changes to an existing WordPress theme, please always work with a Child theme. The procedure to create one is very simple. I'll show you how to do this later on in this chapter.

There's much, much more, like the `comments.php`, `search.php`, `author.php`, and `category.php`. Note that you may use these kinds of different content types, but they aren't mandatory. If you want to learn all about these files, we highly recommend reading a book on WordPress Theme Development. Another great online resource is the WordPress codex: `http://codex.wordpress.org/Theme_Development`. It's also good to have a closer look at the template hierarchy, that describes exactly how all the files in a theme are working together: `https://developer.wordpress.org/themes/basics/template-hierarchy`.

The image below shows a simplified structure of the way in which a WordPress theme is set up:

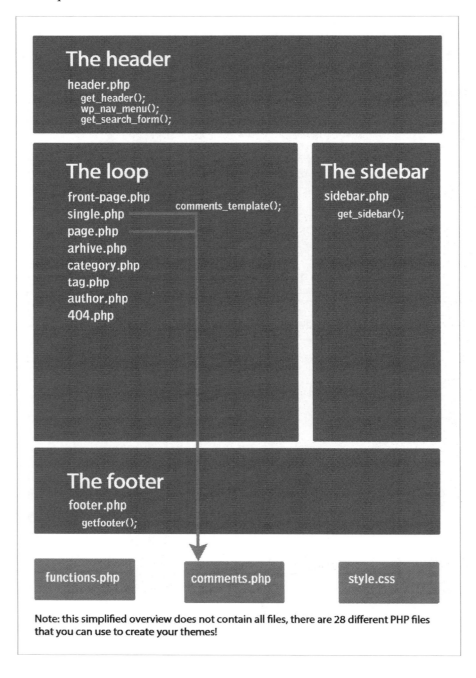

Creating a Child theme

Before making any changes to your theme, it's always good to work with a child theme. A Child theme inherits all the functions from the parent theme that it belongs to. This has the following benefits:

- Everything you changed is easily visible. You won't keep on searching for that one little change that you made, but cannot remember where.

- When your theme receives an update, your changes are safe. The update is applied to the original theme and not to the changes that you made in your Child theme. Do not underestimate this, updates will be there, and only by creating a Child theme, you'll be sure that your changes will not be overwritten.

- It speeds up your web development. Even later on, if you'd decide to create your own theme, it's good to start with a solid base theme and work from there.

The steps that you need to create a child theme for the Storefront theme are as follows:

1. Navigate to the `wp-content/themes` folder. In there, every installed theme has its own folder.

2. Create a new folder named `storefront-child`. If you're creating a Child theme for a different theme, just replace storefront with your theme name. The result should look as follows:

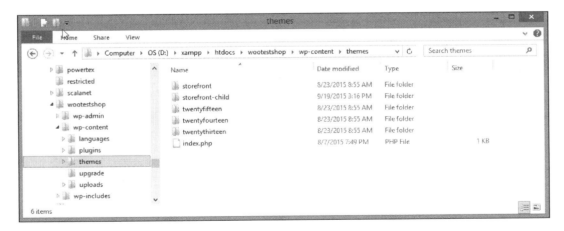

3. In the new folder, create two empty text files named `style.css` and `functions.php`. Use text editor tools like the ones mentioned at the beginning of this chapter.

4. Next, add the following code in the `style.css` file:

```
/*
Theme Name:    Storefront Child
Theme URI:     http://www.woothemes.com/storefront/
Description:   Storefront Child Theme
Author:        Robbert Ravensbergen
Author URI:    http://www.joomblocks.com
Template:      storefront
Version:       1.0.0
License:       GNU General Public License v2 or later
License URI:   http://www.gnu.org/licenses/gpl-2.0.html
Tags:          black, white, light, two-columns, left-sidebar,
right-sidebar, responsive-layout, custom-background
Text Domain:   storefront-child
*/
```

Of course you should replace the various lines with your own data. Important are the lines with the Template name, which is the name of the parent theme folder.

5. We also need to add a few lines of code to `functions.php`:

```
<?php
add_action( 'wp_enqueue_scripts', 'theme_enqueue_styles' );
function theme_enqueue_styles() {
    wp_enqueue_style( 'parent-style', get_template_directory_uri()
. '/style.css' );
}
```

6. It's important to know that if your parent theme loads more than just a single `style.css`, you need to include the additional CSS files separately, just like in your parent theme.

7. Save both the files, and activate the new Child theme in the WordPress backend:

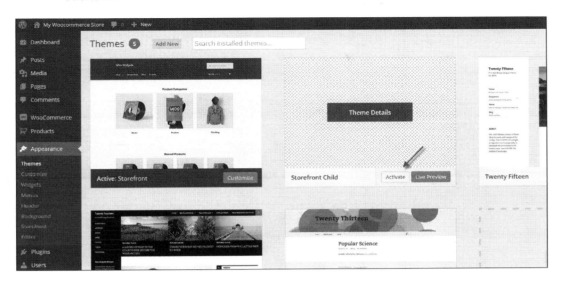

Note that the Child theme exists, but does not have an image yet. You may copy the existing image from the parent theme to your child theme folder (named screenshot . png), or create your own.

Your Child theme is now fully up and running, and you can continue to make changes to it.

Note that the functions . php file of your Child theme will be loaded before functions . php of the parent theme. This gives possibilities to override functions in the parent theme, but only if they have been declared correctly in the parent theme. Do not duplicate function names from the parent theme in your child theme. That could cause fatal errors and your website could stop working completely.

Template files like for instance page . php, single . php, and others can be copied from the parent theme to the child theme. This will overwrite the original file, which gives the possibility to create your own version of these files.

Often, you do not need to change the template files of your theme. Being able to change the CSS using a child theme is already a huge benefit. Let's finish with a simple example. In our Storefront theme, we would like to have a smaller header. The current header contains a lot of white space, which we want to decrease, as shown in the following screenshot:

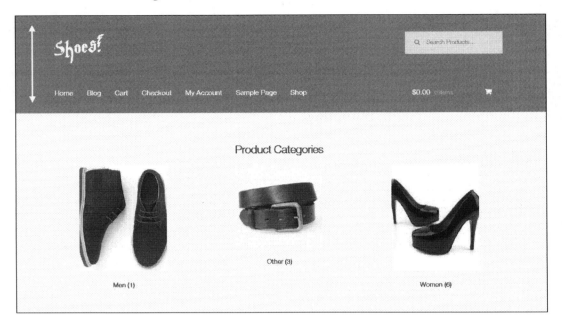

To do that, we simply inspect the elements in the header using the Chrome tools that we saw earlier in this chapter.

We can see that margins have been defined for the site logo in the class site-logo-anchor. There's also a margin at the top of the site header and navigation. Add the following lines of code to style.css of your Child theme:

```
.site-header {padding-top: 1.3em; }
.site-header .site-logo-anchor { margin-bottom: 0; }
@media screen and (min-width: 768px) {
    .main-navigation { padding-top: 0; }
    .woocommerce-active .site-header .site-header-cart { padding-top:
0; }
}
```

All that we do here is use smaller margins and paddings. The last two lines of code will only be applied on desktop screen resolutions (larger than 768 pixels in width). We leave the mobile view unchanged for now. Save the file and check the results. Notice that the header is much smaller now:

Developing WooCommerce themes

WooCommerce is delivered by default with a number of page templates that are used to display all shop information in the correct way. Even using the standard Twenty Fifteen theme, the WooCommerce pages already look pretty good. Just adding some additional CSS might be enough for you to get WooCommerce working even on a theme that was never even designed to work with WooCommerce. If you want to go further than that, here are the things that you need to know:

- As mentioned, do not change an existing theme directly; it's better to work with a Child theme. Using the method described previously, you can be sure that your changes will not be overwritten in case of an upgrade of the WooCommerce plugin.

- Find the default WooCommerce templates in `wp-content/plugins/woocommerce/templates`.

- An overview of all the available WooCommerce template files can be found here as well `http://docs.woothemes.com/document/template-structure/`.

- Copy only the ones that you'd like to change to your child-theme in `wp-content/themes/child-theme-name/woocommerce`. Make sure to place your files here directly; do NOT use the templates subfolder that you can see in the original WooCommerce folder! If you are making changes to an existing WooCommerce theme, you'll already have this structure in place in your Parent theme. In that case, copy the files you want to change to the `woocommerce` folder within your Child theme.

- Keep the subfolders intact. For example, if originally the `price.php` is stored in `wp-content/plugins/woocommerce/templates/single-product`, the location of your changed version of the file should be `wp-content/themes/child-theme-name/woocommerce/single-product`.

- Besides the theme files, the `woocommerce/templates` folder also contains a subfolder holding e-mails. You may copy and change these in the same way to your Child theme to be able to adjust the content of the e-mail messages.

- Simply add/change HTML and PHP in the correct files, depending on your needs to influence the end result.

- A good presentation about the methods described above can be found at `http://www.slideshare.net/corsonr/wordpress-montreal-meetup-woocommerce-templates`.

WooCommerce CSS

WooCommerce comes with default CSS styles to give the necessary elements at least some styling. These CSS files can be found in `/wp-content/plugins/woocommerce/assets/css`. Also here, it's better not to change the existing files because your changes will be overwritten in case of an update of the plugin.

You may simply add some CSS styling to the stylesheet of your Child theme in order to change the colors, fonts, and so on. The stylesheet of your child theme should be made available here: `wp-content/themes/my-child-theme/style.css`.

For example, use the following code to change the color of the buttons:

```
a.button, button.button, input.button, #review_form #submit {
background:green; }
```

If you want to completely disable the WooCommerce CSS styling, you can do this in the following way. Use your theme's `functions.php` file and add the following:

```
add_filter( 'woocommerce_enqueue_styles', '__return_empty_array' );
```

But remember that as a beginner, it's easier to change existing styles than to create everything from scratch.

WooCommerce hooks, actions and filters

WooCommerce heavily relies on the usage of Hooks, Actions, and Filters. It gives you the possibility to override the default output of WooCommerce. For instance, if you want to take control of the Checkout page and add or even remove fields in there, hooks and filters are what you need.

Let's first explain this concept. Within the WordPress and WooCommerce code, developers added hooks. On a hook, you can hang your own code so that it changes the original behavior. There are two types of hooks, which are actions and filters:

- An action allows you to add functionality to WooCommerce at a specific point in the process
- A filter allows you to intercept and change the data as it is being processed

In other words, using actions you can do something and using a filter you can change the data.

If the topic of using hooks and filters is still new to you, here you may find a good tutorial about it: http://wpcandy.com/teaches/how-to-use-wordpress-hooks. Another good read explaining the concept for non-developers can be found at http://docs.presscustomizr.com/article/26-wordpress-actions-filters-and-hooks-a-guide-for-non-developers.

Now, let's take the following example. In some countries, having the **State** field on the checkout page doesn't make sense because **States** are not actively used. In such a case, you might want to remove the field from the checkout page. Here's how to do just that.

Add the following code to your functions.php file in your Child theme:

```
// Hook in
add_filter( 'woocommerce_checkout_fields' , 'custom_override_checkout_fields' );

// Our hooked in function - note that the $fields is passed via the filter

function custom_override_checkout_fields( $fields ) {
    unset($fields['shippping']['shipping_state']);
    unset($fields['billing']['billing_state']);
    return $fields;
}
```

So what does this do? First of all, we add our own custom function to the WooCommerce Checkout fields filter. In our custom function, we simply remove two fields by using the `unset` function. However, please note that this is an example only. Removing the **State** field might break extensions that rely on it. Besides that, the preceding code does not check if the fields are set before removing them. So, be careful when applying changes like these and always make sure to keep a backup copies of the original files available.

There's more to discover regarding the development of your own WooCommerce theme; especially, when working with hooks and filters. Here are some additional resources to move forward:

- `http://docs.woothemes.com/document/third-party-custom-theme-compatibility/`
- `http://docs.woothemes.com/document/tutorial-customising-checkout-fields-using-actions-and-filters/`
- `http://www.skyverge.com/blog/`

Adding a logo using code

We saw earlier that adding a logo to the Storefront theme can be accomplished using an additional plugin. However, such a plugin might not be available for other themes. Besides that, adding more and more plugins is not a good idea for performance reasons. A simple change can just as well be made by a small code change. Let's see how we can add a logo to the Storefront theme without using the plugin. If you installed and used that plugin earlier, please remove it first:

```php
/* Add a logo in the header */
add_action( 'init', 'storefront_logo' );
function storefront_logo() {
  remove_action( 'storefront_header', 'storefront_site_branding',
    20 );
  add_action( 'storefront_header', 'storefront_display_logo', 20
    );
}

function storefront_display_logo() {
?>
  <a href="<?php echo esc_url( home_url( '/' ) ); ?>" class="site-
    logo" rel="home">
    <img src="<?php echo get_stylesheet_directory_uri();
      ?>/images/logo.png" alt="<?php echo get_bloginfo( 'name' );
        ?>" />
  </a>
<?php
}
```

We also need a small change to the CSS of our child theme because the class used is slightly different compared to the one used in the plugin:

```
.site-header .site-logo { float: left; margin-bottom: 0; }
```

Leave the remaining part of `style.css` unchanged. Note that the result of this small piece of code is the same as the one that the plugin offered.

Removing the sidebar

The Storefront theme offers you the possibility to show the sidebar on the right or on the left. But what if you would like to show the sidebar on the category pages, but completely remove it on the (single) product page?

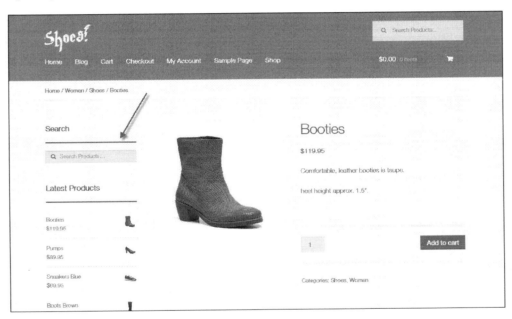

This is also pretty simple to do. With only a few code changes, we'll have more space available for our product images. Add the following to `functions.php` of your Child theme:

```
add_action( 'get_header', 'remove_storefront_sidebar' );
function remove_storefront_sidebar() {
  if ( is_product() ) {
    remove_action( 'storefront_sidebar', 'storefront_get_sidebar',
      10 );
  }
}
```

Next, also add a line to `style.css`:

```
/* remove sidebar on product page */
body.woocommerce #primary { width: 100%; }
```

The end result is a much cleaner product page with larger product images:

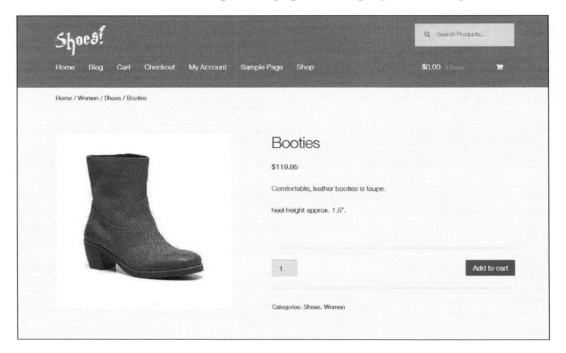

Summary

In this chapter, we've seen the basics of a WordPress theme. Besides this, we've had a look at the specific functions that WooCommerce adds on the top of that and how you can take advantage of the template files included in WooCommerce.

In the next chapter, we'll focus on running our store and working with orders and customer data.

7
Running Your Online Store

During the former chapters, we've learned to work with WooCommerce themes. We even had a look at changing our WordPress theme, although this is a subject that requires a deeper knowledge of web design and coding techniques.

Once we set up our store, payment methods, products, and theme, we are able to start doing business! But what happens next? As a store owner, it's important to test the purchase process completely. Not only to check what your customers will see and receive, but also to know what will happen once your first orders start rolling in. In this chapter, we'll learn to:

- Adjust the notification e-mails
- Deploy our WooCommerce store
- Work with sales orders
- Manage the inventory
- Look at the available sales reports

Adjusting the notification e-mails

Assuming that, up to this point, you've been setting up your store in a development environment, you're now almost ready to deploy your store.

A topic that we didn't fully discuss during *Chapter 1, Setting Up WooCommerce*, is e-mail messages. We discussed the basic settings, but what if we wanted to do additional changes? Let's first go back to the WooCommerce Settings page and click on the **Emails** tab.

Under **Email Options**, there's a link available that shows a preview of your current e-mail template. We added a logo during *Chapter 1, Setting Up WooCommerce* and changed some of the colors. Our example currently looks as follows:

Note that, besides the general e-mail settings, every e-mail that WooCommerce can send has its own form with settings. You may use this to disable the e-mail completely or change its subject and title.

 WooCommerce seems to offer an invoice possibility because it shows a couple of settings for the invoice e-mail. However, real invoice numbering doesn't exist in WooCommerce. WooCommerce uses post ID's, which means in practice that gaps will appear in your order numbering. In lots of countries, it's mandatory to use a progressive invoice number. You'll need an additional plugin to solve this issue. An example will follow in *Chapter 8, More Possibilities Using Plugins*.

If you like to have complete control over your e-mail templates, you have the following two possibilities:

- Use an additional plugin that give the possibility to create the layout of the e-mail templates using drag and drop
- Change the code of the default WooCommerce e-mail templates

In this chapter, we'll take a look at the second option. To be able to change the existing templates, you need to copy the template files to your own theme. By doing so, you will be able to change the HTML of your e-mails completely! Of course, you must have some PHP and HTML knowledge to be able to understand and change the files.

Don't just change the original WooCommerce e-mail templates in the plugin folder because, in that case, your changes will be lost when there's an update of the WooCommerce plugin.

If you want to use this possibility, copy the e-mail templates that you want to change from the following folder:

```
wp-content/plugins/woocommerce/templates/emails
```

Copy this to your theme folder:

```
wp-content/themes/your-theme-name/woocommerce/emails
```

In our demo store, using the Storefront Child theme, this would be as follows:

```
wp-content/themes/storefront-child/woocommerce/emails
```

WooCommerce has a handy function available that copies the necessary file for you. You can find it at the bottom of every individual e-mail settings screen:

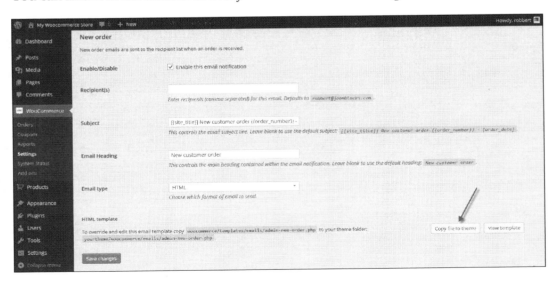

When you copy the file to your theme, it will automatically be added to your child theme if you're using one. Next, the view template button shows the code of the template file. It's possible to make changes here immediately and save your changes. Working that way isn't recommended though, because a small mistake in the code might break your website:

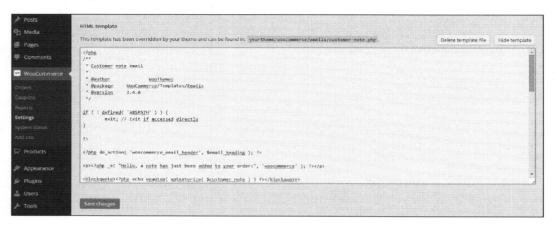

If you made any mistakes that break your e-mail, it's always possible to restart. Use the button Delete template file to remove it from your theme, and you can copy the original file again.

Note that you only need to copy the files that you want to change. Don't just copy all of them if you don't need it. That would only become confusing in the future when doing updates.

In the WooCommerce plugin folder, you'll see a PHP file for every e-mail template. There's also a subfolder available named plain. In this folder, the templates for non-HTML e-mails are stored. Depending on the changes that you're making, it can be necessary to copy as well the HTML e-mail templates as the plain versions to your theme folder.

Besides the template files, there are also helper files like email-header.php and email-footer.php. If you want to make a change to these parts of your e-mails, you need to copy these files as well.

For more information, refer to http://docs.woothemes.com/document/template-structure.

Deploying your WooCommerce store

Once you've set up your store, added products, and changed e-mails if needed, you're ready to start the deployment process of your store. Assuming that up until now, you've been working in a development environment, there's one more important thing that you need to do before bringing live your online store: test it!

Just use your store as if you are a customer. Is everything clear for the visitor? Are the links to conditions and shipping information easily available? Is it clear what payment methods you're offering? But above all, does the order process work? It's very important to spend some time in your own store and actually create orders yourself. So you are sure that it is working and that the e-mails that the customer receives are clear and correct.

If everything is okay, you can start the deployment process. There are many ways to deploy a website from development to live, but, in this example, we use a basic, simple technique to do it. Note the steps below only work if you're deploying a new website. If you are adding WooCommerce to an existing website, other steps could be needed.

1. Create a copy of the WordPress database. Actually, you should do this regularly for every website that you own or are developing. A tool like PhpMyAdmin may be used to create the backup. If you don't know how, also a database backup plugin can be used: `https://wordpress.org/plugins/wp-db-backup/`.

2. If you're developing locally, you'll already have a complete file set of your WordPress installation available. If your temporary site is hosted with a hosting provider, you first need to create a full backup. Use an FTP tool like FileZilla to create one. Or you could even use a WordPress plugin to create a full backup.

3. Next, restore the backup that you just created to the hosting environment at your hosting provider. Again, using FTP with FileZilla is an easy and straightforward method to do this:

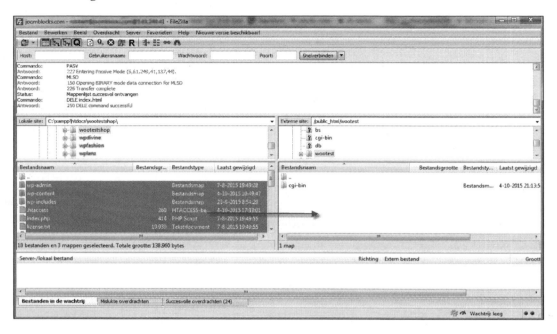

4. Restore your database backup using the Import function of PhpMyAdmin, which is offered by almost every hosting provider.

5. Change the setting in your `wp-config.php` so that it holds the correct values for accessing the database at your hosting provider. If you make changes locally, be sure to upload the file using FTP again.

6. Basically, your store should be working now. However, settings and the contents of sidebars might be lost. This is caused by the way WordPress stores its data in the database. The complete URL, including the domain name, is stored. This is an issue because now that your store is live, the domain name has changed. To correct this situation, we need to do a find and replace in the database so that it will hold the correct domain name in all the records. There are several methods to do this, but I recommend using the tool of InterconnectIT: `https://interconnectit.com/products/search-and-replace-for-wordpress-databases/`. Download the tool and upload it to your hosting environment. Use it to do a search and replace from `http://localhost/...` to `http://yourdomain.com`. Click the **Dry run** button to test the result, and use the **Live run** button to confirm and save the changes:

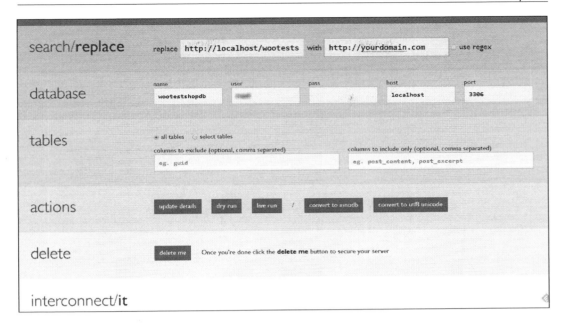

After doing these database changes, your online store will be available on the new domain. Test if it is reachable on your domain, and also test if you can reach the WordPress administrative panel of your site. If something went wrong, your site won't be available. In that case, restore your database and start again.

 If you need more information about moving your development website to a live environment, you may find a tutorial including more details on my website: http://www.joomblocks.com/ moving-a-wordpress-website.

Working with sales orders

Now, we will create a couple of sales orders using our own details just to test the process, whether our payment methods are working, and if the e-mails that we're sending are all working as expected.

An order can be created as well from the frontend as from the WordPress administrative panel. Your customers will order from the frontend, of course. After creating an order, a typical confirmation page will look as follows. Besides the information shown on the screen, the customer and store owner will also receive an e-mail:

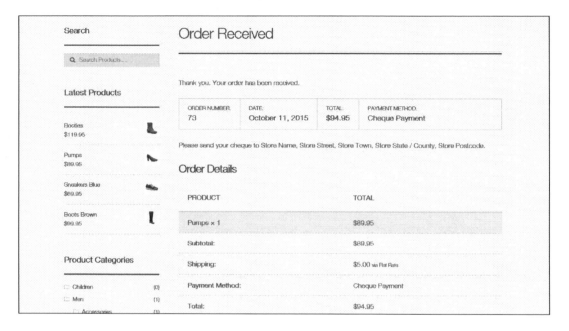

Once we create a couple of orders, we can find them in the WordPress administrative panel by navigating to **WooCommerce | Orders**. You will be notified of new orders directly in the menu. A small circle behind the **Orders** submenu shows the number of new orders:

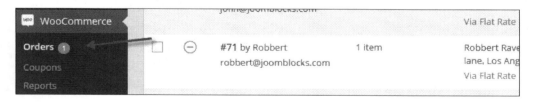

The **Orders** screen shows all the sales orders that you received, regardless of their order status. From here, you may continue to process your orders.

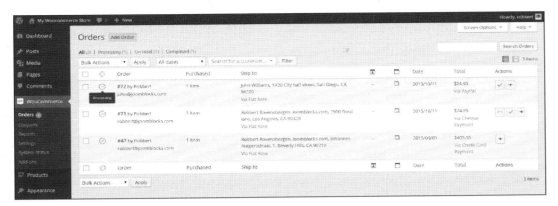

Note the following points when working from this screen:

- The status of the order is indicated by an icon. It's important to pay attention to this so that you won't ship any orders that have not been paid for. A green icon with the dots means that the order status is processing and you may ship the items. If the icon is orange, the status is pending payment. This happens when an online payment method was used, but the order has not been paid yet. An order with a grey icon is on hold and neither has been paid. It might be paid offline by a bank transfer or cheque. Do not ship the order yet. You need to manually check if you received the payment. An icon with a red cross means that the payment was canceled, failed, or was fully refunded; this order should not be delivered.

- You can change the status of the order by clicking on the icon at the right of the order line. For orders that have been cancelled, this isn't possible here. If you still need to change a cancelled order, you may do that by opening the order and edit it from the **Edit order** screen.

- By selecting multiple orders, it's possible to change the status of them all at the same time. Be careful because you could easily delete multiple orders using the bulk function at the top of the screen. Accidentally deleted orders will be moved to the trash and can be restored.

- To the right of the shipping address, an icon will appear if the customer left any additional notes for its order:

- You can look at the order details by clicking on the order number or on the **View** icon at the right of the order line:

The order detail screen shows a lot of information. You can find all the address information, details of the products ordered, including attributes, and detailed tax information. On the bottom right of this screen, you'll find a list of **Order Notes**, holding all the status changes and other information about the process that this order went through. It's possible to add manual notes yourself. There are two types of notes. Customer note will be sent to the customer by e-mail. Remember that these e-mails will only be sent if they are enabled. Navigate to **WooCommerce | Settings | Emails | Customer note** to verify that. It will be visible as well when the customer looks at the order details by logging in again. A private note is for you or your employees only. Your customer will not receive a private note by e-mail.

Further, on the top left of this screen, it's possible to change the **Order status**. You can set it to completed for instance once you have shipped all the items. Unfortunately, it's not possible to only ship a part of the order! After changing the status of an order, you must click on **Save** on the top right to make sure that the status change is actually saved. Depending on your e-mail settings, WooCommerce might send out a message to your customer to confirm that the order has been completed:

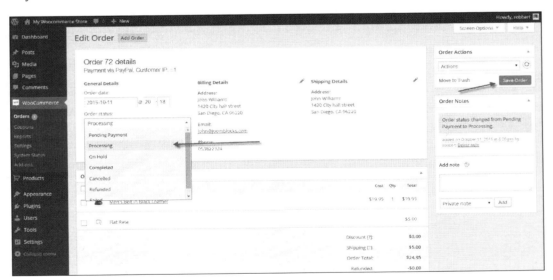

Note that when setting an order to refunded by changing the status on the top right, there's no direct connection to your payment gateway. You'll have to manually make sure that your customer receives back the paid amount. Most payment service providers offer a function to refund an order amount. However, there's a function available that lets you automatically refund the amount online. To do this, use the **Refund** button below the order details. Whether or not you are able to refund the amount automatically depends on the payment gateway. Using PayPal, for instance, it is possible to do an automatic refund.

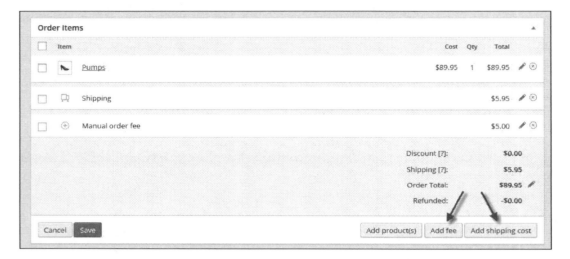

 Handling refunds can be overwhelming sometimes, and there are lots of possibilities. If you want to learn more, there's a good article available in the WooCommerce documentation at https://docs.woothemes.com/document/woocommerce-refunds/.

By using **Order Actions** on the top right, it's possible to manually resend the order e-mails to your customer again. Also in this case, you need to press the **Save Order** button or the **Apply icon** on the right to actually send the message:

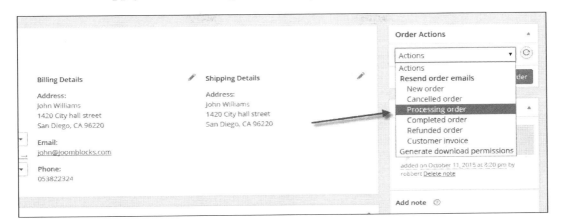

 Note: the **New order email** will go to you as the shop administrator and not to the customer. The **Processing order email** will go to your customer.

At the bottom of this page, there's one more function available. When selling digital goods, like for example e-books, the buyer receives the order confirmation including a download link as soon as the status of the order becomes **Processing**. Sometimes, it's necessary to overrule the default behavior of WooCommerce and grant access to the file manually. You can do that, and it's even possible to grant access to a digital file that wasn't at all on the order. If you want to do that, just type the name of the product in the search box, select the correct product, and click on **Grant Access**:

After giving access, it's possible to limit the number of downloads for this file or set an expiration date. It's also possible to **Revoke Access** again.

After creating several sales orders, you'll notice that the sales order numbering isn't always sequential:

Multiple order numbers are sometimes skipped. This is caused by the fact that WordPress saves everything as a post. A page is a post, a product is a post, and sales order is a post. They all use the same, single number sequence and that's why the sales order numbers will not be sequential. There's a plugin available that can solve this issue at https:// wordpress.org/plugins/woocommerce-sequential-order-numbers/. This is the free version which is working fine but doesn't give you any options. The premium version is available on WooThemes.com.

Adding manual sales orders

Besides handling orders that were created by online customers, it's also possible to manually add a sales order yourself in the WordPress administrator. This is useful for orders that are for example placed by telephone, e-mail, or fax. Situations like this especially appear in business-to-business environments.

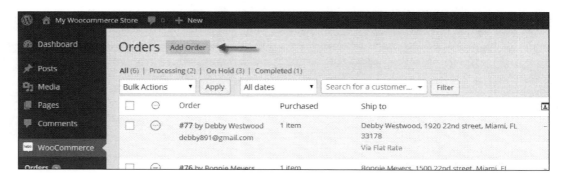

You may select the details of an existing customer by just start typing your customer's name in the **Customer** field. It's also possible to create the order for a **Guest**, so a customer that does not have an account in your store. This is the default setting. In this case, you have to enter the address details manually:

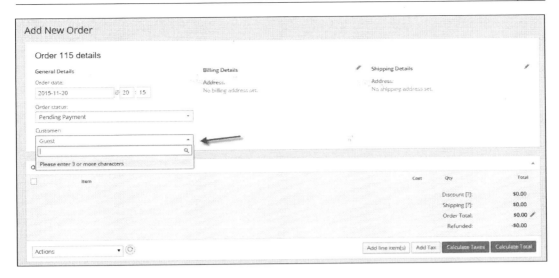

If you want to use the data of an existing customer, start with typing the name in the **Customer** field. Otherwise, keep the default setting as **Guest**.

When adding the address data, the drop-down fields like **Country** and **State** can be filled easily. Just start typing in the field and the matching records will appear:

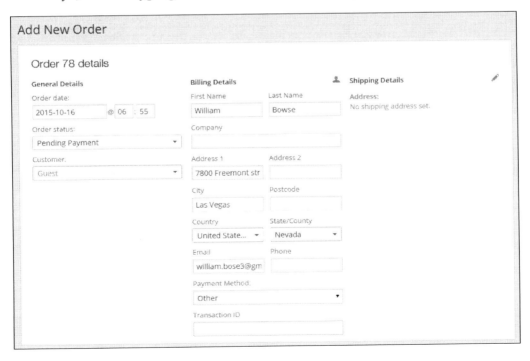

Set **Order Status** and **Payment Method** based on the way the customer is going to pay for the order. When adding **Shipping Details**, it's possible to copy all the data from **Billing Details** so that you do not have to enter them again.

Click on the button **Add line item(s)** button, and then, click on **Add product(s)** to start adding products to your orders:

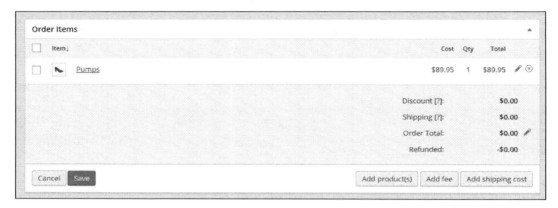

Next, a search window opens that lets you search and add a product to the order. You may change the quantity if needed.

From the window shown in the preceding screenshot, you may **Add shipping cost** to your order or add an order fee using the **Add fee** button. If you're adding the shipping cost, you manually have to select the correct shipping method and amount it will not be filled in automatically.

Click on the **Save** button on the bottom left once you're finished with adding items. Click on **Calculate totals** as well to set the total order value.

Don't forget to also click on **Save** on the top right corner to save your order. Once saved, you can manage this order in exactly the same way as a sales order entered by an online customer.

 The WooThemes website is a great and updated resource. If you have additional questions about managing your orders, then this is a good starting point: `https://docs.woothemes.com/document/managing-orders/`.

Reporting

By navigating in the main menu to **WooCommerce | Reports** we'll be able to take a look at the reporting capabilities that WooCommerce has available. It delivers a number of standardized reports that already give a lot of information. But unfortunately, there isn't much flexibility in this area. Just use what is available or find alternative reporting methods. More on reporting possibilities will follow in the next chapter.

When opening the reporting page, we'll see four main areas that are divided by tabs:

- Orders
- Customers
- Stock
- Taxes

Sales reports

Every main area contains several reports. By default, the reporting section always opens with the **Sales by date** report of the last seven days. The following reports of sales orders are available:

- Sales by date (default)
- Sales by product
- Sales by category

- Coupons by date

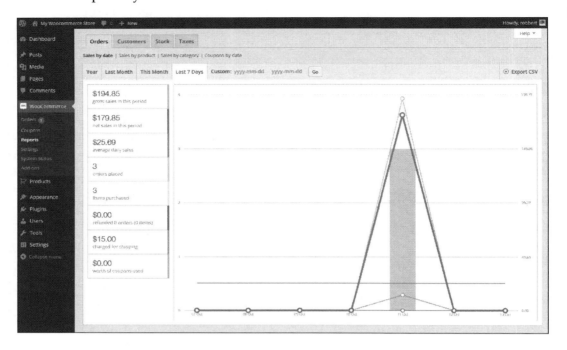

For every Sales report, it is possible to select the date range. By default, this is the **Last 7** days, but other possibilities are **This Month**, **Last Month**, and the **current Year**. Besides that it's possible to enter a custom date range. Click on the **Go** button after entering the start and end date. WooCommerce automatically selects a matching period so that the graph can be drawn. For instance, when selecting a period of a year or more, WooCommerce will show the revenue per month in the graph.

On the top right of the screen, there's a button named **Export CSV**. If you click it, a file will be created holding the data of your graph so that you can import it to, say, for example Excel. Note that this is already aggregated data per period and no individual sales orders will be exported here.

Customer reports

In the **Customers report** section, two reports are available:

- Customers versus guests
- Customer list

The customers versus guests reports give the ratio of buyers that did and did not create an account in your store. The second report, customer list, is more interesting because it shows your top buyers. Unfortunately, customers that do not have an account in your store will not be shown on this list.

Stock reports

There are three different stock reports available:

- **Low in stock**
- **Out of stock**
- **Most Stocked**

All three reports are generally the same; the only difference is the filter that determines which items will be shown:

The example above shows the **Most Stocked** report, which sorts all the products with the available stock. The highest stock level shows on top of the report. You may navigate to the product details in as well the frontend as backend by using the icons on the right.

Stores working with lots of products will have an issue with the limitations of these reports. It isn't possible to export the data or search within the report.

Tax reports

The **Taxes** area contains the following reports:

- **Taxes by code**
- **Taxes by date**

It shows the sales tax that has been calculated for your orders. For both reports, you can set the date range. The **Taxes by code** report splits the sales tax per code, which is handy if you're working with different tax rates for your products. The **Taxes by date** report shows the tax totals per month, regardless of the used tax codes.

Summary

In this chapter, we've learned how to adjust the notification e-mails that are generated by WooCommerce. Next, we deployed our store from a development environment to live.

We also had a closer look at the possibilities to manage your orders. Finally, we worked with the reporting possibilities that are available within WooCommerce.

In the next and final chapter, we'll expand the functionality of our online store using additional plugins. We have covered the basics now, but using plugins there's much more that WooCommerce has to offer.

8
More Possibilities Using Plugins

As you know, WooCommerce is a plugin for WordPress. Even though it might sound strange, it's possible to expand the functionality of WooCommerce with additional plugins. Those are regular WordPress plugins as well, just like any other. The only difference is that these plugins will only work if WooCommerce has been installed.

In this chapter, we'll discuss the following topics:

- Where to find the right WooCommerce plugins
- Popular and useful plugins. We'll have a closer look at:
  - WooCommerce and Google Analytics integration
  - WooCommerce and the Yoast SEO plugin
  - Plugins for advanced products
  - Plugins for online marketing
  - Plugins for easier store management
  - A store in multiple languages
  - Free plugins

Where to find the right WooCommerce plugins

We already noticed earlier in this book that we probably need additional plugins to support the Payment Method or Payment Service Provider of our choice. There are a number of websites that we can check to see if the functionality we need is available:

- **WooThemes**: `http://www.woothemes.com/product-category/` `woocommerce-extensions/`. The extensions offered here are not always developed by the WooCommerce core team, but by third-party programmers. The plugins found here are of a good quality, but sometimes can be pricey. However, note that programmers will have to make some money as well. By charging an amount for their plugins, they will be able to keep supporting them, which is important if your online business is going to rely on it. The commercial WooThemes plugins include one year of support.

- **WordPress**: `http://www.wordpress.org/extend/plugins`. The plugins offered here are free, or have at least a free (limited) version available. We found extensions to support Payment Service Providers and for easier shop management. We'll discuss a few of the free plugins later on in this chapter.

- A valuable resource for commercial, but affordable plugins is **CodeCanyon**: `http://codecanyon.net/category/wordpress/ecommerce/WooCommerce`. In here, you may currently find over 700 (!) extensions for WooCommerce. But pay attention: not all of them will be up to date and ready for 2.4, the newest version of WooCommerce. Just as on ThemeForest, CodeCanyon is a marketplace offering extensions from lots of different developers. Carefully check the given ratings and comments by other users . Not every plugin is supported by the developers. If the support is poor, it's very likely that you can find comments on the support and code quality in the comment section:

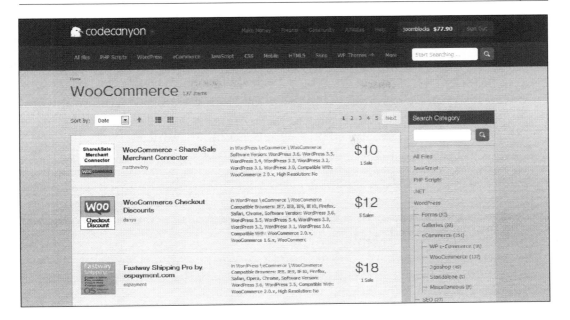

- Other smaller vendors worth checking out are as follows:

    ○ **IgniteWoo** (`http://ignitewoo.com`) is a smaller company which offers themes and plugins.

    ○ **SkyVerge** (`https://www.skyverge.com`) is offering a versatile collection of WooCommerce plugins and also offers some free plugins. The premium plugins of Skyverge are sold on the WooThemes website.

Besides these resources, there will be other developers offering their products and services. Not all plugins are mentioned on the websites mentioned above. If you cannot find what you're looking for, give Google a try as well. There are developers delivering WooCommerce plugins directly from their own website. If you're looking for an extension to support your Payment Service Provider or Carrier, don't forget to ask them if they have one available! Sometimes, you might even get it for free in this way.

Whatever plugin you choose to use, there are a couple of best practices that you need to pay attention to when working with plugins:

- Try to minimize the number of plugins that you're using. Too many plugins can be bad for performance if they are not well-coded. Having too many plugins also makes it difficult to technically manage your shop in the future.

- Have a look at the latest update date. This is especially important for free plugins and plugins offered on a marketplace like CodeCanyon. Is the plugin brand-new, then it might not be the best solution to use in a production environment. If the plugin is not being actively maintained anymore, then try to look for a better alternative. Even if the plugin is still working at this moment, problems will arise in the future when new versions of WordPress and WooCommerce are being released.

- Check the reviews of other users, if available.

- Always make sure that you have a full backup of your website available before you start to add or remove plugins. The backup must include a copy of the WordPress database.

A closer look at plugin prices

When looking closer at the plugin prices, you may notice that some plugins require a yearly renewal, whereas others deliver free updates forever. Vendors change their pricing model sometimes, but, at this moment, you have to take the following into account:

- At WooThemes, you buy the plugin at the full price. After a year, you may renew your license at 50% of the current sales price. If you do not renew, you will no longer be able to download the updates.

- At CodeCanyon, you receive free updates as long as the plugin is being maintained by the developers. Six months of support is included in the purchase price. If you need to extend support, you must pay an additional fee. Be aware that to be able to just download the latest version, it isn't necessary to extend the support period.

All other vendors have varying pricing models and their own way of handling support and updates. Always take a close look at the conditions so that you know what you are going to pay in the future. Keeping your store up to date is important, so please do not stop paying for your extensions just to save some money.

Note that all the prices mentioned in the remaining part of this chapter were the actual prices at the moment of writing. The prices of the mentioned extensions are subject to change.

Popular and useful WooCommerce plugins

Now that we've seen where to go for WooCommerce extensions, which ones will be useful to our store? Although WooCommerce already offers all the basic functions for an online store, there's always something that we can improve or need to do differently.

WooCommerce and Google Analytics integration

Once your store is up and running, it's important to start working on improvements. To be able to do that you first need to collect data about your visitors. Google Analytics is the free and most widely used tool to do so. If you've ever run any website before, you're probably familiar with it.

Unfortunately, even if you have already connected your website to Google Analytics, it will not track e-commerce conversions. Since that is important to have available, we need to take additional steps to solve this issue.

By searching the WordPress.org plugin repository, some plugins are available, but none of these have been actively maintained at the moment of writing.

Therefore, a good combination is the Google Analytics plugin of Yoast (free) combined with the WooCommerce add-on ($49) from `https://yoast.com/wordpress/plugins/ga-ecommerce/`.

When working with commercial plugins, you'll often find that the plugin cannot be installed by searching the WordPress.org repository from the WordPress administrative panel. On a website like WooThemes.com or CodeCanyon.com, you buy your product and receive a ZIP archive in most cases. Such an archive file contains everything that you need, but you first need to extract (unzip) it before being able to use the plugin. The archive often contains the plugin along with documentation and sometimes, other resources. If you don't extract the files, uploading the complete ZIP archive to your WordPress installation will simply fail. If you need more detailed instructions, you can find them on my blog at `http://www.joomblocks.com/how-to-install-a-commercial-wordpress-plugin`.

WooCommerce and the Yoast SEO plugin

During the last couple of years, the Yoast SEO plugin has, more or less, become the standard SEO plugin available. It's the expertise of the Yoast team on the SEO subject combined with a very user-friendly plugin that makes the plugin so popular. The free version gives more than enough options to start. Use them like you're used to for regular pages and posts.

Below you'll see an example of using the basic fields of the Yoast SEO plugin:

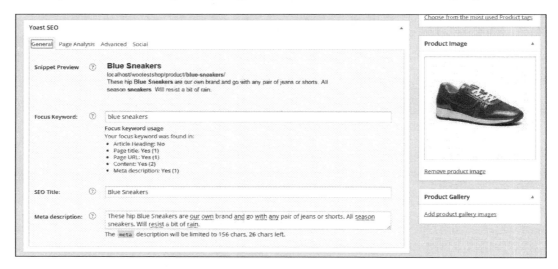

Yoast also offers a paid extension for WooCommerce, which gives some additional possibilities to influence the Twitter, Facebook, and Pinterest integration. It also gives you control over the WooCommerce default breadcrumbs and improves the quality of your sitemap. More information can be found at `https://yoast.com/wordpress/plugins/yoast-woocommerce-seo/`.

The following screenshot show the additional settings the paid SEO for WooCommerce extension is offering:

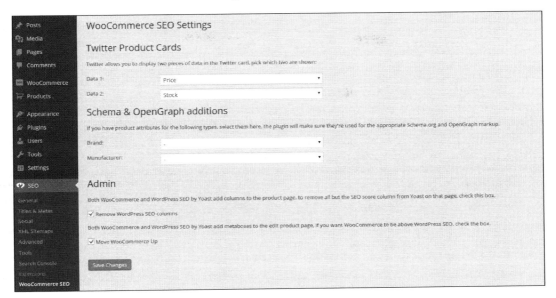

Note that to be able to use **Schema & OpenGraph** additions, you first need to create attributes for your products. After creating attributes for Brand and/or Manufacturer, you'll be able to use them in the WooCommerce SEO plugin as shown in the screenshot above. Refer to *Chapter 3, Using Downloadable Products and Variations*, for more information about working with attributes.

Advanced products

WooCommerce already provides you with some pretty good possibilities to create different types of products, but sometimes, this isn't enough. If you need more options, have a look at the following plugins.

WooCommerce product add-ons are available from WooThemes for a current price of $49. It gives you the possibility to add custom fields to your product, for example, when you need your customer to add a text to customize a product:

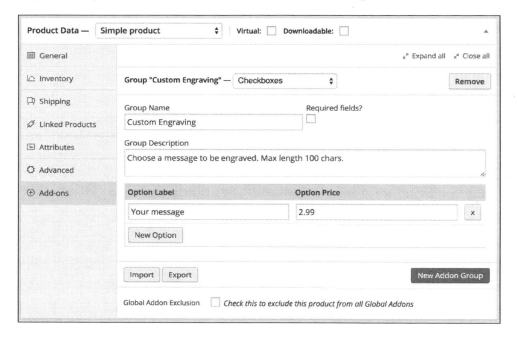

Alternatively, the CodeCanyon plugin, WooCommerce custom fields & Product add-ons, has a similar functionality. On top of that, using this plugin it's also possible to gather additional information from your customer during checkout. The plugin is available here: `http://codecanyon.net/item/woocommerce-custom-fields-product-addons/11332742`.

Another possibility to change fields on the checkout page, if available through WooThemes: `http://www.woothemes.com/products/woocommerce-checkout-field-editor/`.

Online marketing

Next, we're going to have a look at some plugins that will help you doing online marketing for your store in various ways.

The MailChimp integration

E-mail marketing is, or should, play an important role in your online business. There are lots of solutions out there, but MailChimp (`http://mailchimp.com`) is a very popular choice because of the free plan up to 2000 subscribers. Using the MailChimp integration plugin, your customers will be able to sign up to your e-mail list when they go through the checkout. Besides this, the plugin also offers a nice widget for your WordPress dashboard that shows the subscriber statistics. Since it is offered on the WooThemes website, we may assume that it will still work with the latest version of WooCommerce. You may find the plugin here: `http://www.Woothemes.com/products/newsletter-subscription/`. The plugin is also able to use the Ecommerce360 functionality of Mailchimp that gives you the possibility to track visitors and customers coming from your e-mail campaigns individually. Currently, the price for this extension is $49. It can also be used to connect WooCommerce to the e-mail marketing provider Campaign Monitor (`https://www.campaignmonitor.com/`), instead of Mailchimp. Both e-mail providers have plenty of functions available. Mailchimp has a pretty good free plan, which makes it easy and accessible for starting sellers.

There's also a cheaper alternative available at CodeCanyon for $19: `http://codecanyon.net/item/mailchimp-for-wordpress/11479536`, which even includes a visual form designer.

Are you working with a different e-mail marketing solution for your newsletters? There's a good chance that there are integration plugins available. Just check the various extension websites and ask your e-mail provider, if needed.

Social coupons

Having the standard social like and share buttons in your store is something that we cannot do without. We could use the default share buttons you see everywhere, but there are better alternatives available. One of them is the Social coupon for WordPress plugin available on CodeCanyon at `http://codecanyon.net/item/social-coupon-for-wordpress/3417466`.

What makes this extension so interesting is that our visitors can share the product page on social media networks to obtain a discount coupon code that they can immediately use. This could be the ideal last step to convince visitors to buy. If products get shared a lot, this will automatically drive new traffic to your store! Below you'll find a screenshot of this plugin working on our demo store:

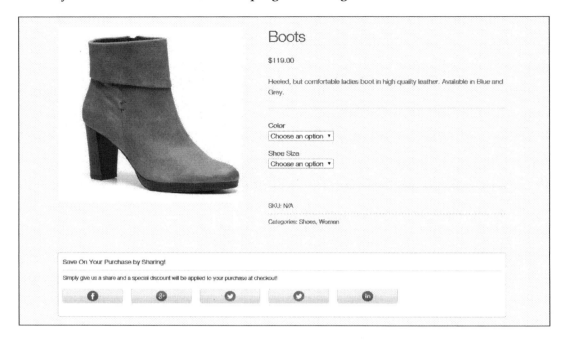

Google shopping

Advertising is going to be important as your store has just gone live and no one will be able to find you through the search engines yet. We recommend having a closer look at this area and learn to use the various possibilities. Besides the well-known regular Google AdWords ads, you could consider using Google shopping as well. More information can be found in Google Merchant Center at `http://www.google.com/merchants`.

You'll need a plugin for WooCommerce to be able to connect the products in your store automatically to Google. You may buy this plugin here: `http://www.woothemes.com/products/google-product-feed/`. It's currently priced at $79 for a single website. There are also other alternatives out there, but for those you need to pay. Free plugins to export your products to the Google Merchant Center are often not maintained.

Alternatively, if you do not have a lot of different products, it's also possible to just fill in a Google spreadsheet with your data and upload that one.

On the other side of the spectrum, we see services like the ones offered by `http://www.exportfeed.com/`. This isn't cheap, but they offer a full service including the possibility to export your products automatically to marketplaces like for instance Amazon and eBay. If you have lots of products and want to be able to sell them everywhere, this is probably a good solution.

Abandoned carts

Lots of visitors on your website will have the intention to buy something from you but, in the end, they don't. Something else came in between and they got distracted. End of story, and you lost your sale. Fortunately, there's something that you can do to help minimize this. There are plugins available that send your customer an e-mail at a specific time after they have abandoned their cart. You could even include a discount coupon in the reminder message.

There are several plugins on the market that help retrieve abandoned carts. Plugins like these will only work if the customer left their e-mail address, for example by creating an account. To name few possibilities `https://www.tychesoftwares.com/store/premium-plugins/woocommerce-abandoned-cart-pro/`. With a price of €119, this is a pretty expensive plugin. Luckily, there's also a light version which is available for free at the WordPress.org website (`https://wordpress.org/plugins/woocommerce-abandoned-cart/`) that gives you the possibility to check the plugin and decide later on if chasing abandoned carts is something that is really going to increase the revenue of your business.

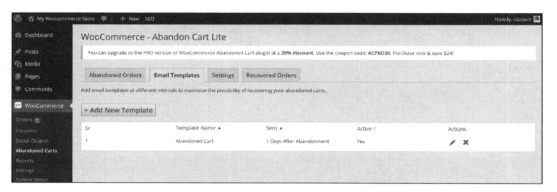

Plugins for store management

There are lots of additional plugins available to expand the functions that are available in order to run store. From shipping calculations to invoicing and reporting, there are extensions available in every area.

Table rate shipping

We mentioned earlier in this book that the possibilities to calculate the shipping costs in WooCommerce are not always enough to suit your needs. Sometimes, you need to be able to store tables with shipping amounts based on volume or weight of the individual products or the total cart. This is where the Table rate shipping extensions will be helpful. There are multiple plugins available on the market. Let's start with the table rate shipping extension offered on the WooThemes website: `http://www.woothemes.com/products/table-rate-shipping/`.

The screenshot below shows you the table rate shipping plugin. In this example, the shipping fee that the customer pays is based on the country and total weight of the order:

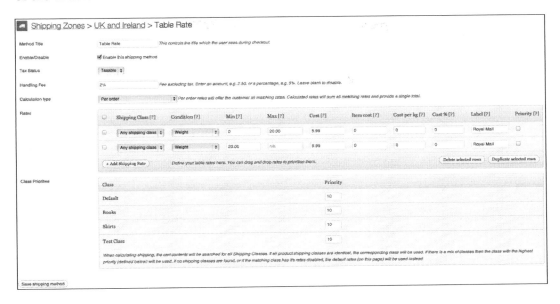

This is a pretty expensive extension with a price of $199 for a single website. The extension is flexible and easy to use, but maybe other alternatives can work just as well. The table rate shipping extension offered at CodeCanyon offers similar functions on a bargain rate of only $22: http://codecanyon.net/item/ woocommerce-table-rate-shipping/3796656. However, note that setting up table rate shipping can become complex. The support offered by WooThemes might therefore be one of the reasons to still choose that plugin.

Note: why would you bother with using an extension from WooThemes.com if plugins found elsewhere are much cheaper? The reason is simple: if you're starting an online business, then you are creating something for a longer period. Extensions bought on the WooThemes store probably will be updated for a longer period. We say probably because, even on WooThemes.com, we won't be sure that extensions will always be updated and continue to be supported. Based on our experience, we expect that your chances are better when using the official WooCommerce extensions, but there are no guarantees. And we've also seen examples of extensions on CodeCanyon that are already available for a couple of years and keep on getting updated. It's up to you to decide.

Invoicing

WooCommerce is offering the possibility to generate invoices for your store, but these won't be valid for all countries. Of course, we have the e-mails that will be sent out, but these are order confirmations only. The PDF Invoices extension available on the WooThemes website does just what we need. It's able to create a PDF invoice and use sequential invoice numbers. The invoice file is automatically attached to the e-mail that will be sent when the order is marked as completed.

The plugin is available here: `http://www.woothemes.com/products/pdf-invoices/`.

The other vendors that we mentioned at the beginning of this chapter are offering invoicing plugins as well. Just check which one fits your needs.

Subscriptions

A function that is often asked for is being able to use subscriptions. Let's say that we would offer access to a closed area of our website with very valuable content. We'd like our customers to buy a subscription in this case and charge them every month. By default, that's not possible in WooCommerce. With the subscription extension, we can do so. This plugin can also be bought at the WooThemes website for $199 (`http://www.woothemes.com/products/woocommerce-subscriptions/`).

To be able to charge customers every month, our payment gateway needs to support such transactions. This isn't always the case. PayPal is supported out of the box by the plugin. For other payment gateways, have a look at this overview: `http://docs.woothemes.com/document/payment-gateways/`.

> Note: More detailed instructions on creating a subscription-based website with WooCommerce can be found in Packt Publishing's book, *WooCommerce Cookbook* by *Patrick Rauland* (`https://www.packtpub.com/web-development/woocommerce-cookbook`).

Reporting

In *Chapter 7, Running Your Online Store*, we noticed that the reporting and management possibilities of WooCommerce can sometimes be a bit limited. And even looking at the available extensions, the choice is still very limited.

The Cart reports extension available on the WooThemes website extends the standard functions with a few additional reports. It delivers interesting information about the number of carts that were abandoned and products that were abandoned while in the cart. If the cart was created by a logged-in user, we can even send them an e-mail about it. The extension is available here: `http://www.woothemes.com/products/woocommerce-cart-reports/`.

Another extension that can get integrated into the reporting function of WooCommerce is the Cost of goods plugin. It gives you the possibility to check your margins by date or product. The extension is available here: `http://www.woothemes.com/products/woocommerce-cost-of-goods/`.

Finally, we would also like to mention the following reporting plugin: `http://woo.report/`. At the moment of writing, this extension could be downloaded for free, but it seems that in the near future, a fee will be charged. This extension delivers some really good insights on customer behavior, sales per product, and value of your stock. These things are missing in WooCommerce itself.

| Orders | Customers | Stock | | | | | | | | | |

Customers vs. Guests | Customer List | New, Active, Returning, Churning, Inactive Customers List | **New, Active, Returning, Churning, Inactive Customers Analytical**

Report is generated with interval type WEEK and last day of week is set as Sunday and considering Sum of Measure in Intervals per type >= or < Threshold, having 1 current interval(s), 2 previous interval(s) displayed out of which 1 previous interval(s) considered, 1 as orders threshold and £50.00 as amount spent threshold. Number of cycles of the report run in the past is 5. Measure(s) considered is(are) Number of Orders. For changing the run-time parameters of the report please visit the settings page of WooReports plugin.

Export to CSV — 5 items

Report run date	New	Active	Returning	Churning	Inactive	Total	New (%)	Active (%)	Returning (%)	Churning (%)	Inactive (%)
2015-08-23	0	0	0	0	7	7	0.00	0.00	0.00	0.00	100.00
2015-08-16	0	0	0	4	3	7	0.00	0.00	0.00	57.14	42.86
2015-08-09	0	0	0	4	3	7	0.00	0.00	0.00	57.14	42.86
2015-08-02	1	0	0	2	1	4	25.00	0.00	0.00	50.00	25.00
2015-07-26	0	0	0	3	0	3	0.00	0.00	0.00	100.00	0.00
Report run date	New	Active	Returning	Churning	Inactive	Total	New (%)	Active (%)	Returning (%)	Churning (%)	Inactive (%)

5 items

Business to Business catalog

WooCommerce can easily be used as an online catalog, but prices will always remain visible. If you want to hide your prices and only show them to authenticated users, this plugin is the one that you need: `http://www.woothemes.com/products/catalog-visibility-options/`.

This plugin also offers the possibility to hide the e-commerce functionality completely so that your store will only be an online catalog:

Importing product data

If we would already have a product catalog available, WooCommerce is not giving us the possibility to automatically import product data. The Product CSV Import Suite available at WooThemes can be a real time-saver: `http://www.woothemes.com/products/product-csv-import-suite/`.

If you are moving from another WooCommerce store, you can just export product data from the first site and import them to the new website using the WordPress importer plugin. In other situations where you have to import your products from another software solution, it's better to use a plugin like the one mentioned previously.

At the moment of writing this, this plugin is priced at $199. You can easily create a CSV file using Google Sheets or Microsoft Excel. If you're currently using a different solution to store your product data, then often there's a possibility to export this data using the CSV file format. The plugin offers enough flexibility to map your product fields to the fields available in WooCommerce.

Alternatively, take a look at the WP All Import plugin at `http://www.wpallimport.com/`.

USA tax calculations

We've seen during *Chapter 1, Setting Up WooCommerce*, that the standard available tax calculations are not always flexible enough when you're doing business in the USA.

The TaxNow plugin, using the Avalara service, can overcome this problem, but it is a paid service. More information about TaxNow can be found here: `http://www.avalara.com/products/avatax`. The WooCommerce plugin can be bought here for $49: `http://www.adipietro.com/product/taxnow-for-WooCommerce/`.

A store in multiple languages

If you need to run a website in multiple languages, there's one major player in the market that you need to go to: WPML (`https://wpml.org/`). Unfortunately, WordPress does not support multilingual websites out of the box, so using plugins is always mandatory. Creating a store in multiple languages is a pretty complex process and requires you to thoroughly read the documentation provided by WPML. You'll need the Multilingual CMS plugin that is currently available from $79. Running WPML can become resource-intensive, so keep in mind that it can have consequences for your hosting plan as well:

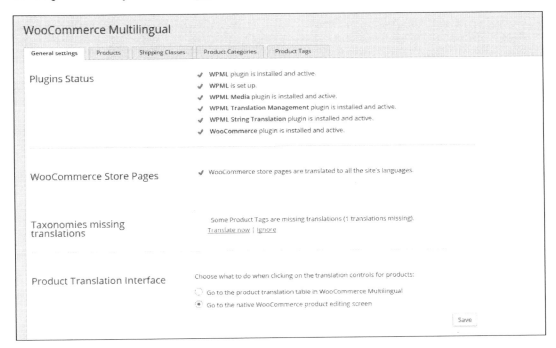

You'll need to install several plugins offered by WPML:

- WPML Multilingual CMS
- WPML Translation Management
- WPML Media
- WPML CMS Nav
- WMPL String translation
- WooCommerce Multilingual

The WPML plugin offers a pretty good guide for beginners at `https://wpml.org/documentation/getting-started-guide/`. Besides that, please also read the documentation the was made for WooCommerce users: `https://wpml.org/documentation/related-projects/woocommerce-multilingual/`.

All the plugins are included when buying the WPML package.

Free plugins

We've seen in this chapter that the majority of WooCommerce plugins are offered by commercial parties. Sometimes, there's a free, limited version of the plugin available. Now, there's nothing wrong with this because if your online business relies on it, it's better to have a developer that is actually maintaining the plugin code. This doesn't mean that with a free plugin the code won't be maintained, but we've seen lots of situations in the past where free plugins were not regularly updated. However, if you're looking for free plugins, here are a couple of examples that are worth checking out:

- The WooCommerce customizer (`https://wordpress.org/plugins/woocommerce-customizer/`) offers a couple of combined functions which are simple but actually missing in the WooCommerce core. You can, for instance, set the number of products shown on the product page and change some of the default texts used within the checkout process.

- WooCommerce does not use sequential order numbers. This is caused by the fact that the numbering is shared with other post types like pages, posts, products, and so on. The result of this is an order number sequence that doesn't make sense at all. This free plugin solves this issue: `https://wordpress.org/plugins/woocommerce-sequential-order-numbers/`. However, test it in your situation first; I've seen examples where the plugin didn't play together nicely with the payment plugins.

- WooCommerce doesn't offer wishlist functionality out of the box. The plugin YITH WooCommerce Wishlist (`https://wordpress.org/plugins/yith-woocommerce-wishlist/`) solves this in a nice way and is regularly updated. There's also a pro version available that is offering more options.

Of course, the plugins mentioned above just were examples to show you what WooCommerce is capable of doing. There are many, many more possibilities, so always carefully check if your requirements can be met using an existing extension. If the functionality that you need is not available, it sometimes makes sense to have it created just for your situation. In such a case, always ask for programmers that have experience with creating custom WooCommerce plugins!

Summary

The functionality of WooCommerce can be easily expanded using plugins. Unless you have a unique requirement, almost everything is already available. Most of the plugins aren't free, but remember that developers will have to be able to deliver continuous support on their products. Although it is tempting to install lots of plugins, we recommend installing only what you really need. The more plugins that you have, the larger the chance of conflicts or problems during WordPress or WooCommerce upgrades.

By now, you should have a good solid knowledge of the possibilities of WooCommerce and the way in which the solution works. Of course, there's more to discover than the topics discussed in this book. The WooThemes website is being updated continuously and is always a good resource for more information. Besides that, continuing with the WooCommerce Cookbook is a good next step as well (`https://www.packtpub.com/web-development/woocommerce-cookbook`). It contains lots of practical WooCommerce recipes for users and developers.

Index

USA tax calculations plugin 164

V

variable products
  setting up 57-65
Virtual products 50, 51

W

web designing
  references 113, 114
  tools, using 115
Webhooks
  URL 29
widgets
  using 93-95
WooCommerce
  about 1
  Accounts Settings Tab 26, 27
  API Settings Tab 29
  Checkout Settings Tab 22-24
  Email Settings Tab 27-29
  General Settings Tab 13-15
  installing 5-13
  Products Settings Tab 15-19
  setting up 13
  shipping settings tab 24-26
  Tax settings tab 20-22
  test store, preparing 30, 31
  URL, for documentation 140
WooCommerce extension
  URL 86
WooCommerce plugins
  best practices 152
  for abandoned carts 159
  for advanced products 155, 156
  for online marketing 156
  for store management 160
  free plugins 166, 167
  Google Analytics 153
  pricing 152
  selecting 150, 151

URL 165
Yoast SEO plugin 154, 155
WooCommerce Sequential Order Numbers
    Pro plugin
  URL 142
WooCommerce store
  deploying 133-135
WooCommerce theme
  actions, using 125, 126
  CSS styling 124
  developing 123, 124
  filters, using 125, 126
  home page, setting up 107, 108
  hooks, using 125, 126
  installing 101-105
  logo, adding 126, 127
  reference link 126
  settings, configuring 106, 107
  sidebar, removing 127, 128
WooTax
  URL 22
WooThemes
  about 97, 150
  URL 97
WooThemeshere
  URL 78
WordPress
  about 150
  URL 150
WordPress theme
  basics 116-118
  child theme, creating 119-123
  URL 31
WP All Import plugin
  URL 69, 164
WPML
  URL 165

Y

Yoast SEO plugin
  about 154, 155
  URL 154

Thank you for buying
Building E-Commerce Solutions with WooCommerce
Second Edition

About Packt Publishing

Packt, pronounced 'packed', published its first book, *Mastering phpMyAdmin for Effective MySQL Management*, in April 2004, and subsequently continued to specialize in publishing highly focused books on specific technologies and solutions.

Our books and publications share the experiences of your fellow IT professionals in adapting and customizing today's systems, applications, and frameworks. Our solution-based books give you the knowledge and power to customize the software and technologies you're using to get the job done. Packt books are more specific and less general than the IT books you have seen in the past. Our unique business model allows us to bring you more focused information, giving you more of what you need to know, and less of what you don't.

Packt is a modern yet unique publishing company that focuses on producing quality, cutting-edge books for communities of developers, administrators, and newbies alike. For more information, please visit our website at www.packtpub.com.

About Packt Open Source

In 2010, Packt launched two new brands, Packt Open Source and Packt Enterprise, in order to continue its focus on specialization. This book is part of the Packt Open Source brand, home to books published on software built around open source licenses, and offering information to anybody from advanced developers to budding web designers. The Open Source brand also runs Packt's Open Source Royalty Scheme, by which Packt gives a royalty to each open source project about whose software a book is sold.

Writing for Packt

We welcome all inquiries from people who are interested in authoring. Book proposals should be sent to author@packtpub.com. If your book idea is still at an early stage and you would like to discuss it first before writing a formal book proposal, then please contact us; one of our commissioning editors will get in touch with you.

We're not just looking for published authors; if you have strong technical skills but no writing experience, our experienced editors can help you develop a writing career, or simply get some additional reward for your expertise.

WooCommerce Cookbook

ISBN: 978-1-78439-405-9   Paperback: 248 pages

Create, design, and manage your own personalized online store with WooCommerce, the fastest growing e-commerce platform

1. Get your online store up and running in no time.

2. Dozens of simple recipes to setup and manage your store.

3. Easy to understand code samples that can help you customize every tiny detail and take your store to the next level.

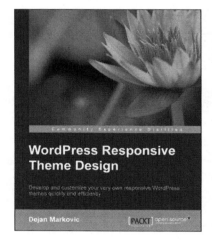

WordPress Responsive Theme Design

ISBN: 978-1-78528-845-6   Paperback: 228 pages

Develop and customize your very own responsive WordPress themes quickly and efficiently

1. Structured learning for new developers and technical consultants to enable you to build responsive WordPress themes.

2. Concise and easy-to-follow walkthroughs of WordPress, PHP, and CSS code.

3. Packed with examples and key tips on how to avoid potential pitfalls.

Please check **www.PacktPub.com** for information on our titles

WordPress Web Application
Development
Second Edition

ISBN: 978-1-78217-439-4   Paperback: 404 pages

Build rapid web applications with cutting-edge technologies using WordPress

1. Develop rapid web applications using the core features of WordPress.

2. Explore various workaround techniques to prevent maintenance nightmares by identifying the limitations of WordPress.

3. A practical guide filled with real-world scenarios that will guide you through how to build modular and scalar applications.

WordPress 4.0 Site Blueprints
Second Edition

ISBN: 978-1-78439-796-8   Paperback: 324 pages

Create a variety of exciting sites for e-commerce, networking, video streaming, and more, using WordPress

1. Build ten different types of website using WordPress.

2. Transfer your static site to WordPress and create sites to make money, build communities, and share your ideas.

3. The projects in the book will teach you how to use free themes and plugins without any prior coding experience.

Please check **www.PacktPub.com** for information on our titles

Made in the USA
Lexington, KY
08 August 2018